Domains is published bi-annually in the United States & Sri Lanka by the International Centre for Ethnic Studies, Colombo, under the editorial direction of Pradeep Jeganathan. In the US *Domains* is published under the imprint, *ICES Colombo*, under an agreement with South Focus Press, New York.

Domains is distributed by Ingram Book Company and Baker & Taylor in the US, Whitakers in the UK, and Ingram International through out the rest of the world. These issues may be ordered from any bookstore in those countries, and is also available from amazon.com. Wholesale orders may be placed with www.ipage.ingrambook.com

Domains gratefully acknowledges the assistance of Trinh Nguyen, Dulani Kulasinghe & Soundari David in the production of this issue.

Domains is a refereed journal.

Domains Three and other subsequent issues are available as books (ISBN: 0-9748839-48, for this issue) and also as a serial (ISSN: 1391-9768) through out the world. Yearly subscriptions rates for first world contries are: Institutions US$ 85.00, individuals: US$ 35.00. Subscriptions for Sri Lanka are SL Rs. 750, and for South Asia and the global South are US$ 15.00 and may be ordered from P. Thambirajah, *Domains* Subscriptions, International Centre for Ethnic Studies, 2 Kynsey Terrace, Colombo 00800, Sri Lanka or via email to thambirajah@gmail.com.

Domains welcomes submissions of between 7,500-10,000 words, from all disciplines of the social sciences and humanities, pertaining to any geographical area of the world. Both purely theoretical and empirically rich articles are valued, if original and rigorously argued; thematically important are problems of subordinate and dominant nationalisms in post-colonial spaces, questions of statehood, rule and governance, conflict resolution and constitutional reform on the one hand and gendered violence and social suffering, cultural diversity and communal co-existence on the other. *Domains* is particularly interested in post-disciplinary intellectual projects such as postcolonial feminism, critical legal studies and subaltern studies. Submissions, which should include an abstract of 150-300 words, should be sent as a MS-Word attachment to submissions@icesdomains.org. For the most current information about special issues and themes visit www.icesdomains.org.

This issue of *Domains* was printed in the United States on acid free paper

DOMAINS

EDITOR
PRADEEP JEGANATHAN
INTERNATIONAL CENTRE FOR ETHNIC STUDIES

•   •

INTERNATIONAL EDITORIAL BOARD

DOMAINS THREE

A Special Issue: March 2007

RIOT
DISCOURSES

Deepak Mehta and Roma Chatterji

(Editors)

CONTENTS

•

Introduction:
Riot Discourses*

Deepak Mehta and Roma Chatterji

The papers in this special issue deal with the category of the communal riot in India, specifically the anti-Sikh riot of 1984 in Delhi, the Hindu-Muslim riots of 1992-93 in Mumbai and the Hindu-Muslim riots of Gujarat in 2002. The literature, both academic and in the print and visual media, on each of these riots is vast, but as yet we do not find a sustained effort to put together these events of violence, much less reflect on their common modalities.[1] The papers in this issue mark an ethnographic attempt to come to terms with what in India (and perhaps the Subcontinent, at large) has been a ubiquitous phenomenon since at least the mid-1980s – a pervasive repetition and visibility of intra-religious warfare. The papers show that the communal riot is both a practice and a discursive condition, anchored in documentary, pictorial, ethnographic, narrative, and judicial accounts. In the process the papers shed light on different dimensions of the riot, while also revealing regularities and diversity in its discursive formation.

Working through an anatomy of detail, each of the papers argues that the riot is not a one-off event, forever estranged from social processes and everyday life. It produces social identities (Yasmeen Arif's paper on widows) and enables a critique from the point of an aesthetic tradition (Mani Shekhar Singh's paper on painting).

---

*The papers in this special issue of *Domains* are part of a project called, 'Mapping City Spaces: Communal Violence, Social Reconciliation and the Documentary Practices of the State.' The project is sponsored by the Indo-Dutch Programme on Alternatives in Development (IDPAD). We wish to acknowledge the generosity of IDPAD in aiding this research and to Dr. Sanchita Dutta of the ICSSR. The research would not have been possible without the team at ISERDD. We thank Lester Coutinho for support and Veena Das for intellectual nourishment.

[1] There are, of course exceptions. Stanley Tambiah, *Leveling Crowds: Ethnonationalist Conflicts and Collective Violence in South Asia* (California: University of California Press. 1996), and Donald Horowitz, *The Deadly Ethnic Riot* (Delhi: Oxford University Press, 2002) use a much broader canvas to discuss the riot.

Working on a separate but related register, the riot as available in documents cross-cuts juridical identities based on abstract right (Pratiksha Baxi's paper on the juridical discourse of the riot), and shows how in the colonial archive the circulation of the imagery of violence comes to influence the testimony of those who have been affected by violence in the present (Deepak Mehta's paper on documents and testimony). Finally, a reading of the riot is available from a perspective that is displaced from the discourse of violence to that of slum redevelopment (Roma Chatterji's paper on slum housing and demolition). A common weave that runs through all the papers is an attempt to address, implicitly and explicitly, the prominence of the state in any understanding of the riot. Taken together, the papers show that the state itself is a multifaceted ensemble of power relations. It is material and mythic, protean and without boundaries, decentered and centralized. In what follows we will schematize the way in which each of the papers negotiates with ensembles of power instantiated by what we call the state.

In presenting the possibility of grievable lives in the face of the violence in Delhi, Arif shows the pathos of *ressentiment* to the extent that the widows she studies express the affects of rage and righteousness. *Ressentiment* here is not the 'moralizing revenge of the powerless' in Brown's use of the term,[2] as much as it is a sense of loss, rage and guilt occasioned by the impossibility of redemption. The fragmentation of previous forms of association, marked by a literal and figurative exile from the site of violence to a relocation colony (some might call this a camp), subjects the widow to a relentlessly public form of mourning and to an effect of domination that reiterates impotence. Listening carefully to their voices, Arif shows that rage and loss are directed not merely at the perpetrators of violence but also the agencies of the state that promised restitution, but in their eyes delivered little. As widows, the trajectory of their lives embodies suffering, not as social virtue, but as eternal reaction.

If the widows are condemned to live a life of reaction, the pictorial narrative of the Gujarat riots that Singh studies attempts to reclaim the ground that has been ceded to the Hindu right. Reading a

---

[2] Wendy Brown, *States of Injury: Power and Freedom in Late Modernity* (Princeton: Princeton University Press, 1995, 66).

series of paintings composed by an artist versed in the Mithila school of painting, but also technically equipped in Western art forms, Singh shows how this artist mounts a moral critique of the Hindu right. This critique becomes possible in the re-situating of some of the traditional icons of Hinduism and their juxtaposition with public figures like Mahatma Gandhi, on the one hand, and Narendra Modi, the Chief Minister of Gujarat during the riots, on the other. The moral and aesthetic representations that Singh considers are a critique of a certain kind of power, a complaint against brute force, an effort to shame and discredit domination by re-appropriating the ground of the good. In this way, of course, the critique itself becomes a weapon, a kind of power that is based on an imaginary revenge.

Both Arif and Singh provide an understanding of power that is framed by intentionality – its effects on the subjective life of widows and an artist's rendition on canvas of the Gujarat riots. Baxi provides a different mode of understanding the deployment of power. Focusing on a series of appellate judgments, Baxi shows that power relations are both nonsubjective and imbued with calculation. The juridico-legislative dimension of the state as it relates to the riot is anchored in the crowd-public dyad. The legitimate and arbitrary power of the state to regulate the riot creates not only a distinction between reason and passion, but also produces a zone of illegality and silence. Baxi reads these silences as the inability of the law to address the gendered violence of the riot. Further, in dealing with the irrationality of communal violence the state places it within the terrain of national security and extraordinary law. This power does not result from the choice of an individual as much as it is available in the documentary practices of the state.

Mehta places these practices within a history of Hindu-Muslim violence in Mumbai and reads the written word in juxtaposition with the oral testimony of a survivor of the riots of 1992-93. Perhaps the most revealing expression of the relationship between the written and the spoken word concerns the use of documents and the rules of evidence. However, rather than present the riot through details of evidence, Mehta shows that the discursive structure of the riots of 1992-93, as available from official enquiry commissions bears a remarkable similarity with enquiry commission reports generated in colonial India. Such documentary practices enter into the inner life of survivors of the riot. In the process, these practices encapsulate the power to fashion individual testimony and remembrance.

While the state seeks to control the meaning of the riot by placing it within a juridical and bureaucratic understanding of communal violence, this ordering is never in the form of a closure. In focusing on the demolition of slum housing in a slum in Mumbai, initiated by agencies of the state and the response of local nongovernmental organizations, Chatterji shows that the bureaucratic dimension of the state is expressed in tangible institutions and discourses. These discourses address the consequences of communal violence. The state's procedural tendencies and its emphasis on expertise constitutes one of several state voices. In discussing the procedures and techniques of slum housing, Chatterji focuses on the problematic of disciplinary power. As far as slum housing is concerned Chatterji shows that rather than working through tight coherent strategies, the policies of slum redevelopment have a contingent ring about them. In part, this contingency is a response to the needs of slum inhabitants and in part is it guided by conceiving of property as commodity. In either case, we find the emergence of solidary groups that are not organized on the basis of religious identities and communal animosity.

A second theme that runs through the papers is an elaboration of 'critical events' – those that 'stick out' from the everyday and have the capacity of re-ordering time and place.[3] Arif shows how the riots of 1984 reorganized the city by creating zones of violence and enclaves of memory such as Tilak Vihar, the colony where the widows were housed. In a different vein Singh looks not at the Gujarat riots per se but to the images of violence that they produced. In an unusual perspective on communal violence Singh discusses the appropriation of media images of violence by traditional iconography. Santosh, the artist who paints in the folk style of Mithila, embeds the event in a cosmological frame and gives the riots a new meaning in

---

[3] See Veena Das, (*Critical Events: An Anthropological Perspective on Contemporary India*. Delhi: Oxford University Press, 1995) and Hans Joas, (*G.H. Mead: A Contemporary Re-Examination of his Thought*. Cambridge: Polity Press, 1985).

terms of sacred time and place. In the process, however, tradition and even cosmology must be reinterpreted.

Both Arif and Singh explore voices at the margins – Singh by focusing on the singular and highly eccentric perspective of a creative artist and Arif through the voices of widows who feel that they have been cast away by the city. Chatterji's paper also configures the margin, but not through the singular event of violence. Instead she explores the dispersal of the event along a different axis by unpacking its different traits. She foregrounds one trait always associated with collective violence – displacement/dislocation – and maps it on other events, such as the state-sponsored demolition of huts in slum areas. In this way she constitutes a different genealogy for the Mumbai riots.

In a seminal essay on the genealogical method, Foucault describes the social world in terms of a 'profusion of entangled events.'[4] The genealogical method studies events in their dispersion. It traces the complex lines of descent to reveal the conditions in which certain events emerge. Mehta attempts a historiography of the riot, juxtaposing commissions of enquiry reports with oral testimony with one of the survivors of the Mumbai riots who testified before the Srikrishna Commission. Mehta does not seek to establish continuities between diverse domains of representation. Instead he focuses on the ruptures between dissimilar registers of representation and experience. Thus, he constitutes the document as a social field in which different actants position themselves in a vast network of power.

How do riots acquire the status of singular events? What allows us to represent multiple events within one overarching frame? We suggest that it is through the act of narration that clusters of incidents acquire the status of a critical event. Official documents, investigative reports and oral testimonies are all narrative acts that contribute to the crystallization of the event of violence. Baxi's paper on the constitution of the riot through appellate court judgments reveals the normative categories through which events and persons are classified as potentially violent. By focusing on the forms of censorship that allow for the creation and circulation of a certain type of

---

[4] Michel Foucault: *Language, Counter-Memory, Practice: Selected Essays and Interviews.* (Ithaca: Cornell University Press, 1977. 155).

representation, she reveals the processes by which some kinds of knowledge are suppressed, thereby producing a kind of agency that can fit the subject of the riot narrative.

The narrative method allows us to explore events over time. This allows us to examine the multiple subject positions that our narrators may adopt and the different temporal registers within which their experiences may be embedded. All the papers in this volume try to examine critical events in new narrative contexts. We use this as a representational device to make problematic the writings on collective violence in India, which more often than not understand the riot through stable classificatory referents.

The Delhi Carnage of 1984:
The After Life of Violence and Loss

Yasmeen Arif

Abstract

This essay is a re-visitation of the 1984 carnage against Sikhs in Delhi, through a framing of its apparent afterlife, in the last two decades. It is an ethnographic depiction of experiences of a group of widows and their families who reside in a relocation colony (The Tilak Vihar Widows Relocation Colony), assigned to them since the event. These experiences are read together with the surrounding discursive universe of state documentary practices, enquiry commission reports and other public representations. While exploring the nuanced afterlives of loss, grief or mourning, the queries that contour the essay are - what kind of subjectivities does the state engender in these kinds of people? what conditions of enablement or vulnerability does 'legitimate' victimhood provoke, especially when justice continues to elude these people? The answers to these explorations lead to the idea of an exile, both in a material and metaphorical sense. It is a notion that allows for these biographies to be grasped as recovered lives that continue within ostensible normalcy, but as identities of those that are forsaken. These are identities that track a course through generations into a future, embedding the burden of memory into the terrain of the future, tainting the realm of hope rather than remaining in the past.

•••

In Poussin's painting, *Gathering the Ashes of Phocion*, Phocion's wife bends down outside the boundary wall of Athens to scoop up his ashes, in an integral *gestus* which gathers her own soul and body into this act of perfect devotion. The tension of political defiance and the fear of being discovered appear only in the taut *contrapposto* of the woman servant, which is juxtaposed to the utter vulnerability of the stooping wife. Arising above the two foregrounded figures is a combined land and townscape of classical magnificence, gleaming temples and municipal buildings, perfect displays of the architectural orders, which convey no hint of malign intent. Yet Phocion's condemnation and manner of dying were the result of tyranny temporarily usurping good rule in the city.

...In Poussin's painting, this transcendent but mournable justice is configured, its absence given presence, in the architectural perspective which frames and focuses the enacted justice of Phocion's wife, her response to the implied act of injustice by the city. To see the built forms themselves as ciphers of the unjust city would be to perpetuate endless dying and endless tyranny – unending disaste.[1]

This essay begins with a few days in 1984, when the seeming 'usurpation of good rule in a city' caused one of the worst carnages in independent India. The assassination of the then Prime Minister Indira Gandhi by her Sikh bodyguards, on the morning of 31st October 1984, had incited an onslaught of violence against the Sikh community in Delhi, the capital city.[2] With genocidal intensity, several Sikh localities in Delhi were targeted and men, both young and old, were annihilated through some of the most grotesque methods of mass murder. Countless women were raped, houses burnt and looted, business establishments and even entire colonies were razed to the ground. This essay describes and attempts to make meaning of the continuing lives of some of those who survived this carnage. These lives are those of the widows and their children who live in the Tilak Vihar Widows Relocation Colony (hereafter the Colony) situated in a dense neighborhood of West Delhi.[3] Tucked away beyond the edge

---

[1] From Gillian Rose, *Mourning Becomes the Law: Philosophy and Representation.* (Cambridge: Cambridge University Press, 1996). "Phocion was a virtuous Athenian general and statesman, who, like Socrates, was sentenced to die by hemlock, and, in addition, refused burial within the walls of Athens." Rose, *Mourning becomes the Law,* 150

[2] The assassination of the Prime Minister by her Sikh bodyguards was connected to the prevailing Sikh militancy. The period from 1st to 4th November 1984 are considered to be the worst 72 hours of the carnage, an event unparalleled in the city since the partition of 1947. Some of other parts of the country were affected as well. Official figures estimate the dead to be 2733, most of them men in the age group between 20-50, although other sources place the figure at 4000 or above. There are yet no official figures of the injured, of raped women or of the houses and businesses looted and destroyed.

[3] The ethnographic information in this essay is based on our interviews with approximately 30 households in the neighborhood. Simi Bajaj and Harpreet Kaur from the ISERDD research team helped me with these interviews. Most of the original

of a bustling, fairly prosperous neighborhood, this is a place which by virtue of its nomenclature and its residents' profile becomes, as I intend to argue, an address of exile. The particular nuance that I would like to draw from the words of Gillian Rose quoted above is this sense of 'cast away-ness' that the residents of the Colony experience, denounced by the powerful 'structures' of the city. Perhaps the lofty city buildings that provide the backdrop for Poussin's painting represents an iconic view of the high ideals of a city-state; an imagined and aspired space that can sustain the honorable governance of a contract between the individual and society, partly mediated by the techniques of statecraft as well as a rational, critical public sphere. Foregrounded against this could also be the Colony residents - forsaken by justice as they perceived it, removed from a 'normal' society they were familiar with and defined by deaths that remain meaningless, they remain outside the scheme of the 'legitimate' order of the city. Two decades have passed since the event and while monetary or material compensation has been the measurable mode of 'justice' offered to the survivors, convictions made against the murders committed continue to be absurdly disproportionate.[4]

The metaphorical 'banishment' to a place is heightened by a loss made private and insular in the lives of these survivors because they perceive their mourning to have failed in achieving formal retribution. By this fact, their loss seems invisible in the formal remembrance of the city. The image of Phocion's wife against the mighty structures of the city in Poussin's painting brings to relief unaccountable death that has to be disregarded, cast outside the limits of the

---

allottees came from two of the worst hit colonies in the city – Sultanpuri and Mongolpuri. There were others from various parts of the city. The variations amongst the families in economic status or social classification in terms of caste groups were significant. This is not a point that I can elaborate here, suffice to note that apart from visible differences in material goods (although the overall colony could be loosely termed lower middle class), there were internal social differences as well which were often mentioned by our informants with reference to caste groups.

[4] A longer discussion on this follows. It is virtually impossible to trace the trial proceedings or exact number of convictions for any given charge filed during the 1984 carnage (or most other case proceedings in India) given the incredibly long time spans and wide geographical dispersal of cases. I have taken recourse to a specific report compiled by Vrinda Grover, *Quest for Justice: 1984 Massacre of Sikh Citizens in Delhi*, (Mimeo, 2002), that investigated a sample of the 1984 cases in order to provide an adequate overview of the state of affairs.

ordered city, which, in turn renders the survivor threatened and threatening. This essay mirrors this portrayal by describing, on one hand, the authority of the state and its institutions in either acknowledging or disregarding disorderly deaths, of withholding or dispensing benevolence/justice. On the other, it is about an afterlife of loss and injustice that constitutes an ongoing vulnerability amongst those who were left behind. If the metaphor of the city were to stand for a conglomeration of the state (as in the Athenian city-state of Phocion's painting), the arenas of the public and those other agencies that come into effect in these circumstances, the subjectivities engendered by the 'city' with reference to un-retributed death suggest a powerful aspect of state practice and its ramifications in taking away individual agency from personal biography and in its place inscribing a seemingly futile future. In the manner that Gillian Rose indicates above, this is an opposing relationship constructed and sustained as an aggravated opposition between the agonies of suffering inside against the seeming relentless injustices of the outside. The discussion is thus about the interstices of the violent event and those who survived it intersect with state practices, justice and quotidian existence. It attempts to trace the metonymic domains[5] of affect that such interactions perpetuate into realms of socialities of these lives and their futures. In another way, it is about how the ordered city/state can perpetrate, through its forms and structures, an unending of the '84 disaster as it unfolds in the future realm of these lives.

Survivors, Perpetrators and Benefactors: Domains of Affect

The relationship of opposition or the engendering of subjectivities in this exploration engages primarily with the figure of the widow and her children. These are figures whose constitutive bodies appear to be split down the middle with the singular stroke of an event of mass violence. One side is made up of an alleged 'enabling'

---

[5] Understood literally, the 'metonymic' domains of affect here point to an assemblage of contiguous emotions and subjectivities that arise amongst the group I have observed, both conceptually and existentially. These are framed by the event but the frame also encompasses the idea of an afterlife – a temporal extension beyond the event itself.

public bureaucratic classification[6] of a victim that counts as an index of entitlement. The other is the stigma and burden of private grief and loss, made acute and apolitical to the extent that it has not found its closure in legal justice.[7] However, it is not the alleged lack of justice alone, but public knowledge that constantly reminds and reiterates this and makes this an 'open,' public wound. There is an ironic twist which causes this wound to be nursed as if it is intensely private, as an internal subjectivity alone but its intensity appears to have been also fuelled by the fact that it is 'known' to be an open wound, as it were, by an outside, by an arena of the 'public.'[8] It is the same reason why the impotency of the outside makes this burden a private one, but yet sustained by a public.

For instance, as per official figures, there were a total of 707 cases filed in relation to the massacre. The following detail about these cases as reported by Vrinda Grover[9] as part of an investigation into the role of justice in the events of 1984 indicates the overall situation.

---

[6] The term 'enabling' as it is used here cannot be understood in its positive connotation alone. By 'enabling' in this context, I am alluding to the brief moment of entitlement that a survivor/victim may find themselves in, as compared to a large number of others who simply disappear from bureaucratic accounting. To have one's loss acknowledged and then compensated does suggest a quasi–enabling moment, when complete hopelessness appears to be the alternate condition.

[7] The lack of legal closure is part of the *after*–life of the event. However, this splitting starts from the first moment of interaction with state practice. Veena Das writes about how the writing of the First Information Report (FIR) by the police during the carnage becomes a compelling illustration of the 'lie' of the state. The FIR, in the first place was required to claim compensation, but was itself was a gross misrepresentation of facts because the police failed/refused to record the repeated incrimination of their own officers or politicians in the massacre. "Thus, ironically, those who were locked in a combative relationship with the state and who had direct evidence of the criminality of the state nevertheless ended up being pulled into the gravitational force of the state through the circulation of documents produced by its functionaries." Veena Das, "The Signature of the State: The Paradox of Illegibility," 229, in Veena Das and Deborah Poole, *Anthropology in the Margins of the State*. (eds.) (New Delhi: Oxford University Press, 2004)

[8] By the public here, I do not refer to any particular discursive concept but rather the entire discursive and empirical range that would include the media, the law, citizen's groups and their activities, state directives etc. that have been formed over time. All of this cannot be mentioned or discussed here in any adequate detail, so I have concentrated on the 'public knowledge' of legal justice as an illustrative category.

[9] Grover, *Quest for Justice*, 75.

Of these, 322 cases were sent as un-traced and cancelled. As many as 320 cases had ended in acquittal. While 25 cases were pending in trial courts, only 30 cases, which did not even constitute 10 percent of the total, resulted in conviction.

It has to be mentioned that most of these convictions are not about the murders but are rather about looting, arson, rioting and so forth. In Vrinda Grover's analysis of a representative sample of 126 Trial Court cases, the following description indicates the general pattern that these cases have taken,

> ... only 8 cases resulted in convictions while the rest resulted in acquittals. Of these 8 convictions, 2 were overturned by the High Court while the death sentences awarded in 3 of the cases were reduced to life sentences by the Supreme Court. In this sample, 99 of the Trial Court Cases relate to the offence of murder under section 302 IPC. An analysis of the judgment reveals a pattern – that a combination of grave lapses in investigation, inordinate delays, insufficient evidence, procedural lacunae led to a majority of cases concluding in acquittals.[10]

Clearly, there has been a 'failure' of law or due process by which the most heinous of acknowledged offences –murder– has remained unaccounted for.[11] However, these murders themselves, by rendering a group of women as widows, gives them and their children a classificatory label – 'victims'[12] with rights of claim to compensation.

---

[10] Ibid.

[11] The Hindu (A National Daily), Tuesday, 17th May 2005 reports that five persons have been sentenced to life imprisonment by a Delhi Court for the murder of Baba Singh. The five men had pulled him out of his home, poured kerosene on him and burnt him alive. This conviction is a recent addition, but, with a time lag of twenty years.

[12] I have used the word 'victim' here because of its usage in the various judgments/court orders and other public documents relating to the 1984 carnage. However, the category of those who survive mass violence has been discussed through tropes of the witness, the survivor, the testifier and the victim. *Vide* Giorgio Agamben *Remnants of Auschwitz: The Witness and the Archive*, (New York: Zone Books, 1999), Ana Douglas and Thomas A.Vogler (eds.) *Witness and Memory: The Discourse of Trauma* (New York: Routledge, 2003), Cathy Caruth, *Trauma: Explorations in Memory* (Baltimore: The Johns Hopkins University Press, 1995). My usage of the term 'victim' here merely replicates the category that is employed both in bu-

Two sorts of material compensation were made available. First, single room apartments in the four storied blocks of Tilak Vihar. All of these houses in the Colony were originally meant to be Grade IV housing for government employees, which were then reassigned as accommodation for these women survivors and their children. Approximately 950 families were given allotments here from around March 1985; around 700 of these were widow families.[13] Monetary compensation for loss of lives had initially been stipulated by the state at a rate of (Indian) Rs. 10,000 (approx US$ 250) per life in 1984. In 1997, this amount was increased to Rs. 200,000 of rupees (approx US$ 2,300) which together with retrospective interest amounted to Rs. 350,000.

It is interesting to note that this increased compensation amount was based on a Delhi High Court judgement which led to a court order that directed the Delhi government to pay the required amount to all the survivors within four months. The judgment states:

> It is the duty and responsibility of the State to secure and safeguard the life and liberty of an individual from mob violence. It is not open to the state to say that the violations are being committed by private persons for which it cannot be held accountable…
> Thus those lives which are endangered or lost during the riots, clearly come under the purview of the violation of Article 21 of the Constitution…. If it is not able to do all that then it cannot escape the liability to pay adequate compensation to the family of the person killed during the riots as his or her life has been extinguished in clear violation of Article 21 of the constitution.[14]

By taking recourse to the constitution, the courts make the state responsible and liable to the survivors and assign a calculable

---

reaucratic or other public terms, because the discussion is more about reiterating how the public-private world of this group is constructed. The emphasis, therefore, is not predominantly about the location of this group in the literature that addresses the constitution of these categories.

[13] Figures quoted from information available at www.nishkam.org. (March 2005)

[14] Bhajan Kaur v. Delhi Administration 1996 III (Delhi) 333. (As cited in Vrinda Grover, *Quest for Justice*)

value to the lost life. Between this and the complicity of the state[15] in dis-allowing convictions for murder lies the future of the widow's life world. For the widow, it is the loss itself that has made possible a quasi-enabling moment, which has created a subjectivity of a claim-ant, in relation to the giving authority (the state or other organiza-tions that demonstrate a capacity to provide some form of support) potentially into the temporal extent of an entire lifetime.

Apart from state compensation, another source was the Delhi Sikh Gurudwara Management Committee which had provided a monthly pension to these widows which has now been discontinued for six years. One of the main non-governmental organizations pro-viding support in the Colony is the community establishment called Nishkam Sikh Welfare Council (hereafter, Nishkam), which has been working in the area since it was established as a Relocation Colony. Apart from providing healthcare and schooling, vocational training and counseling to young people of the Colony, it also maintains a Sewing Center which started with the main aim of providing some form of livelihood for the widows. One of the dominant themes in many of our conversations with the Colony residents has been the kind of everyday support received from various sources, or rather regarding its current lack. A consistent complaint has been the changing nature of Nishkam and how their intentions have changed from charity to profit making even in such essential areas as health-care.[16] The tone of these complaints always posits an underlying sense of 'right' to the facilities that Nishkam has to offer. Nishkam officials however maintain that it is quite impossible to continue the initial kind of support for 20 years, suggesting that nothing is quite enough when the 'habit' of entitlement sets in.

In addition, there is a substantial amount of talk about eve-ryday facilities like water and electricity which supply, like in other similar localities of the city, remains illegal and sporadic at best. The

---

[15] Apart from popular knowledge, various Citizens' reports have categorically docu-mented the manner in which the police in conjunction with powerful politicians or-ganized the riot. The failings of the police or their co-operation with the perpetrators and the subsequent mishandling of case procedures is a significant part of this.

[16] For example, we were told how a renowned film star and parliamentarian Sunil Dutt had gifted an X-Ray machine to Nishkam. X-Rays are however only available at a price to the residents.

Colony residents report how some bills show up from time to time, none of which are ever paid because, as they say[17]

> (Elderly widow A): They had said they will give us a house in place of a house. My man was killed, my brother was killed, my whole family has been killed – for what reason should I pay a bill. We said bring our men back, we will pay our bills. We do not have jobs, work, we have small children... how are we to educate them, feed them? Even our little ones have to go and earn.

There continues to be insecurity about the houses as well, for instance,

> (Elderly widow B): They have fixed Rs 42,000 for these houses. The government has allotted but they have not paid their dues to the DDA.[18] Only when the government pays up will our houses be free... They ask us for money – sometimes a notice shows up. They should make a concrete decision on this. Today, I am alive. Tomorrow when I die, they will throw my children out because our allotments are still uncertain.

This kind of material insecurity stems from a deeper affect, from an experience of failed justice that extends, in my opinion, from this seemingly mundane everyday terrain to a more negative interiority, one that ties in the outside, the public to the private and the local.

> (Elderly Widow B): Whatever has happened to us was very bad. What can we do now? What has happened to us has happened. But then, even our Guru Granth Sahib has been desacralized. What has been done to our men has been done. Our Sardars have always been martyred. We are a community of martyrdom, but Durbar Sahib has been burnt – it has been vandalized. What fault did it have? Many Gurudwaras have been burnt. The people who had done this, their killings, nothing has been done. Nobody has been caught. There are these hearings and then our people say, 'well, this government

---

[17] For lack of space, I will not include biographical details on each informant here; The names of informants are not mentioned in order to protect their privacy.
[18] Delhi Development Authority. All government housing in the city comes under its purview.

is supporting us.' No government is supporting us. We are just sitting peacefully, waiting for when God will Himself act. …We do not want anything from them, the justice we should have been given has been denied to us.

…Whatever has happened in whatever way, the Sikh Community has forgotten everything. They have forgotten everything – they garland those people, today our murderers have won and come back and our brothers are garlanding them. There is no one to listen, no justice. They gave us jobs but with the jobs our children were left behind, no one to look after them The children kept going wrong without us…when women leave their children behind, what can happen, they will go wrong – under whose care could we have left them. No one child here has been reformed – some are drug addicts, some gamble. Our community should have settled us – the Gurudwara has stopped our pension – they say, your children are now earning – they have done nothing for us. They have done whatever they wished. They might go on making Prime Ministers, but till we do not get justice we will remain tormented like this. Now we do not want to talk about all this. When we don't get any justice in our own home – those homes where 10 men were burnt, what will be our condition. …

Go to Nishkam, they tell you – forget '84. How can we forget, even if a dog in the house dies, we are sad. We have lost our young children, our world has burnt with them. 12 men, we are just waiting for them to come home, we are waiting and on the way, petrol is poured on them and they are burnt.

Our living is not living.

At the time when these narratives where recorded, during 2004, the Congress party had returned to power with a startling and sweeping victory, and ironically, with a Sikh Prime Minister. As the woman's narration above suggests, destiny and time has worked to seal their misfortune because the perpetrators of their misery have returned to power. This betrayal is not just about politics; it is also about a community that has appeared to have 'forgotten' the gravity of 1984. Thus, it would seem, intertwined in these stories is a mingling amongst and between the party and the politician, the state and its executives, the community and its institutions, all pitted against a loss. A loss that remains without retribution because justice in the sense of attaining legitimacy to loss has remained unattainable, relegating it to not just to the inner domain of personal pain but also as a social frustration, a community betrayal. Left alone, so to speak, to carry the burden of injustice, it seems that the energy required to fuel this sense of this injustice comes not only from the private trauma but also the incessant reminders of it.

Simultaneously, in the lives of these women, healing cannot come easily because of a double bind that renders the state both enabler and perpetrator through the dynamics of the same event. These women bear the knowledge, in their daily remembrances and their narratives, that the state perceived in the form of the police or the politicians have been responsible for their loss. At the same time, it is the state itself that becomes the only meaningful benefactor because their attempts at reclaiming a life are made possible by the largesse of the state in giving them an idea of entitlement. It is a strange facing off of subjectivities, of conditions of affect that the state seems to initiate, which in turn haunts these biographical trajectories as they unfold into everyday corporeal life.

I do not suggest that a conviction is the only form of justice that these women would have found acceptable or would have liberated them from their sense of victimhood. Rather it is a 'public' and 'private' subjective personhood that the lack of legitimate death engenders in these women, the morass of meaninglessness of their loss that makes them believe in their state of diminished existence. It may not be hazardous to describe these phenomena in these survivors as a situation that sometimes provides some recourse when faced with one's own inadequacies. Although the limitations of this essay does allow a deeper exploration of the experience of coming to terms, of rebuilding lives, I do not find enough analytical comfort in rendering these biographies as entirely without succor. In another sense, there is some sense of recovery that such lives clearly manifest, however it is the peculiar entanglement of the public and the private and its intersection with state practices that makes a sense of victimhood more acute, or more permanent. Because there is another side to this story – some in the colony, arguably very few, have indeed remarked on the fact that the 'habit' of receiving under the label of victimhood have rendered the colony into an irresponsible society attuned to entitled deserving rather than to earning. Nonetheless, it would not be correct to represent my ethnographic findings in just one way, and although not explored in this essay, the possibility of life going on by whatever means is and has to be a part of this discourse. My representation of these phenomena should not arrest these biographies as I suspect some of the issues I describe here have.

However, what remains striking is that the condition of affect moves far beyond the lifetime of a single generation. In fact, it seeps invariably into a future, seemingly encompassing temporality within its grip of futility. It could be said that the 'unending disaster' is most poignant at the level of the young. While it remains implicated in the narratives of the elders, the sense of doom becomes literal amongst the young - a few instances of these are apparent in our conversations with some young men of the Colony, illustrating how far into the future this double bind continues. These young men are between the ages of 19-24. Most of them were infants or very young during 1984 or were born soon after.

> A: We have not received any support from the government. They had said that they will give you these things, they will give your children jobs, they will make your children stand. They have done nothing....

> Sometime ago there was a fire in a cinema hall in the city. The government has given them a lot, they are still giving them a lot. That was an accident. But with us, it was done to us, still they give us no help. With us it was no accident, it was done to us. The government should have once thought, there were riots, let us look at them – do they have all facilities or not. There is nothing here. They send 2-3 people – they talk to the leader here and that's all.
> ...Its twenty years since 1984. But the government has not thought of keeping 15 seats for the children of the '84 people. They have not done anything till now.

Flowing underneath, in the same breath, was also an undercurrent of revenge:

B:...But, the day we get our turn, this is just a matter of opportunity, those people took advantage of the situation, the mistakes of the police...

A: ...you know what kind of mistakes these police made. All of our people had come together, do you know what the police said? No fights are taking place, go home and leave your weapons with us.

B: Never mind a day, if we could get just an hour. They had three days. They should give us an hour and see. The day we get a chance we will show them. The community can say what they like, but anger inside never dies. Those who can kill their own and win cannot be considered manly (*namard*). I cannot live like that. What are the sardars doing these days? There is no sardar now who has any humanity – in spite of them showing their piety. Tytler has come again to contest – the man who killed our fathers, burnt them alive, he is again being put up. Why do the sardars have no courage, couldn't they have shot this Tytler, this Sajjan. Why are they standing again? They only keep fighting behind the Gurudwara.[19]

Clearly, these narratives are domains of affect, reproductions of those expressed by their mothers, ones that are peculiarly produced and reproduced in time and space through these biographies. These are the instances that illustrate the relationships of subjectivity that the metaphorical city/state bring about, particularly when there is usurpation of good rule and whose reminders are not made to go away.

Beyond the Limits of the City: Addresses of Exile

These generations in the colony, both past and future, are now a 'community' of victims bound together by their common loss and grief to follow a common destiny, remembered on occasion as anecdotes in another discourse of yet another 'similar' event in the country. But their lives have continued for twenty years of ordinary living in one way or another. What is the nature of this life? Have these lives been assigned any proper political subjectivity? Did their loss make for a 'grievable life,' i.e. a public political existence that

---

[19] B is referring here to Jagdish Tytler and Sajjan Kumar, both prominent Congress politicians who had a number of cases filed against them. However lack of evidence and other procedural irregularities have prevented any concrete outcomes. Fighting behind the gurudwara implies the internal politics within the religious authorities.

moved into the realms of justice, closure or any form of retribution?[20] Have they been blended back into some form of cohered social fabric? If from Judith Butler's idea of a grievable life, I am to understand the legitimacy of their widowhood, their entitlement to legal or to any other kind of right, then the widows of the Colony do not have grievable lives. Their grief and mourning is the continued private trauma and memory (constituted 'publicly' as well) that constitutes the other part of the widows' entity. It is this other part that reproduces itself into a terrain of exile, as I suggest below.

It may be said that the Sikh widow of 1984 is not just a post-facto figure after 1984, in the discourse that surrounds her. The history of Sikh militancy[21] that preceded 1984 could also suggest a vulnerability to this community of women who could have had no other outcome but to eventually become a 'community' of widows. There appears to be a terrible legacy that condemns these women to a life of loss even before the loss could occur. They bear the cross of a political and violent struggle that bore the sign of the entire historic group of Sikhs which has left its scars on some, not all, from amongst the community and on behalf of them. As victims living in a city who could not or did not exercise the option of 'returning' to or finding shelter in some other refuge like a family home in order to remake their lives, they became a constructed community within a beleaguered community.[22]

This is a community not only in physical exile from the familiarity of their known 'secure' past homes, but they are also in exile from a certain sense of personhood, or, in another way, in their sense of womanhood. The 'masculine' militancy of the Sikhs could be thought as a preemptive condition for this community of widows, a preceding vulnerability. I would also maintain that this is a vulner-

---

[20] Judith Butler, *Precarious Life: The Powers of Mourning and Violence* (London: Verso, 2004), 19-49.

[21] See Brian Axel, *The Nation's Tortured Body: Violence, Representation and the Formation of the Sikh Diaspora*, (Durham: Duke University Press, 2001) amongst others, for an overview of the Sikh militancy and its historical background.

[22] I would emphasize the fact that while it is indeed the Sikh 'community' at large that suffered this attack, the burden of its afterlife is different within different sections of the community depending on a variety of factors. This has very significant implications in understanding the afterlife of an event of this proportion. Later, in this section, I will discuss an aspect of this with regard to another neighborhood in Delhi explored with similar queries.

ability that extends to the younger generation by the very virtue of being a part of the widow's[23] world – a world (and a word) that is made up of an acute relationality to others, the men, whose loss and absence reduces them to a life of incompleteness, a life of eternal lack. The women are incomplete insofar that they are widows rendered so unnaturally and violently, a fact that does not gain them a 'whole' right. Even during the brief temporal span when they became the rightful claimants to compensation, their legitimate claims to the monetary relief they were offered had its own vagaries. Community prescription decreed that the widows were in fact only partial claimants because the money had to be divided equally with the dead men's fathers.[24]

In addition, their children are to be always fatherless and therefore somewhat lesser than other 'complete' youth. The young men speak with the grief of their mothers and the passion of their youth, while the young women live surrounded not by men who can offer protection but those who themselves threaten or are threatened. These are not circumstances that are born out of a 'common' misfortune of death or poverty but they are afflictions that are caused, conditions that have an externality in blame. These are not changeable conditions that could be or are meant to be dealt with by personal or social means. In fact, they are impediments to the movement of biography because they remove even a consciousness of agency from private life.

At another level, there seems to be a temporal bracketing to the colony as well, one that removes these lives from 'ordinary time' to a 'limited' temporal frame with a very distinct moment of origin.

---

[23] Widowhood in India does establish itself as a special social category, a 'community' on whom very stringent social control is often practiced. For an exploration of widowhood in rural India, see Martha Alter Chen, *Widows in India* (New Delhi: Sage, 1998) and *Perpetual Mourning: Widowhood in Rural India*, (New Delhi: Sage, 2000). The generally disadvantaged life of the widow, in the larger context of Asia and Africa is explored by Margaret Owen, *A World of Widows* (London: Zed Books, 1996). The notion of political widowhood is somewhat closer to the Sikh widows, insofar that the deaths of these men become a sort of symbolic capital of a community which is used politically. It also throws up issues that interface a personal loss against a public death. An example of political widowhood is Mamphela Ramphele, "Political Widowhood in South Africa: The Embodiment of Ambiguity," *Daedalus* 125(1), (1996): 99-117.

[24] Veena Das, "Signature of the State," 229 –230.

During our first visit to the Colony, we met a group of widows in the stitching center maintained by Nishkam. While trying to introduce ourselves and the purpose of our interest in their lives, we took pains to elaborate how we did not want to reopen old traumas, we did not really want a retelling of the event; rather we were interested in their lives after, in the ways they coped and continued with their lives. As we discovered in that first visit and in the subsequent first meetings with a majority, the narratives were inevitably anchored around a beginning and that point was the days of the event. In seemingly accurate recall, most told us about the way in which the mobs appeared, how they ran through alleys, through houses trying to find places to hide. They described how they tried to hide their sons, fathers or husbands, they remembered the ways a father was beaten to death, how little boys were burnt in heaps, how young men were cut up and left to die. In whatever multiple trajectories the narratives took after that initial moment, it seemed significant that life as constructed by these narratives bound, even stopped time, within the limits of the event. It would seem that temporality, in these biographies, do not spill out beyond the limits inscribed by the event. The future appears trapped as an afterlife of the event itself rather than as a accumulated unfolding of time.

In trying to make meaning out of these initial moments of the narrative, the desire in these women to start the conversation with a vivid recollection of the event itself and moments of tragic horror suggests the following. Did the past for them only start from that one event, and no remembrance is possible unless it starts from that one point which becomes an anchor on which hinges the possibility of remembrance? This point comes into sharper focus when it is juxtaposed against similar recollections that I could elicit in Bhogal. [25] In Bhogal, the recollection of the past extended into a different kind of anchor, a different kind of excavation of the past. While some de-

---

[25] Bhogal is the second neighborhood in Delhi that we had explored for the same research agenda. Bhogal however, is not a relocation colony. It is a predominantly Sikh neighborhood that was attacked during the carnage, but there was no loss of life. One of the main reasons ascribed to this is that the community in the neighborhood itself could come together quickly to put up a far stronger physical resistance. However, very substantial damage to property and businesses was incurred. Many homes and shops were burnt – goods carrying trucks, which were a main trade amongst the residents, were destroyed.

tailed the events of 1984 in the way they unfolded in their immediate neighborhood, most founded this event through a historical loop that brought together their community with the Partition and 1984. We were told that the Partition was an attack by those 'others,' but this time it was the neighbors themselves making the latter event doubly tragic. Survival and triumph over the second episode was just a matter of time. For most in Bhogal, '84 and beyond was the triumph of a proud, hardworking, noble community whose ability to survive is just an echo of another time, of another experience. This is a very different kind of community experience of memory in the present than the experience in the Colony. Two parts of a community who had undergone the same tragic event, (notwithstanding the difference in their experiences in terms of the losses) yet their excavation into their past from the vantage point of today differs. What sets them apart?

I am persuaded to understand this separation in the community through a separation of the notions of loss, grief and mourning. If in Bhogal there is a notion of triumph over a history of persecution, the future of their memory, as it were, of past events is a narrative of recovery, of reclaimed normalcy. Their utterances of reclaiming a life emanate from notions of a hardworking, noble community whose ability to triumph over their tragedies is readily apparent in the way they have been able to replenish their losses. Most have been able replace the trucks that were burnt, rebuild the house that were destroyed and recover the businesses that were interrupted. In Bhogal, material loss has been compensated by material recovery there appears to be an apparent sense of equitability between the before and after. Normalcy is restored through a kind of substitution.

In the colony, on the other hand, there is no retribution, no lost life has been replaced by a life taken in conviction. The widows in the colony, on the other hand have been suspended in 'futile' mourning, as Butler[26] might suggest, because their compensation has not replaced their fundamental loss of life.[27] That in itself extends the

---

[26] Judith Butler, *Precarious Life*, 19-49.
[27] This brings out a important difference between life and property and their implication in reclaiming worlds after devastation. I intend to focus on this in a later essay.

grief into a future, or the past extends to a future which does not yet provide any tangible sign of recovery in the public personhood of the widow. In so far that there has been no retributive formal justice for the violence committed against them, their grief remains illegitimate, or in Butler's[28] terms, they do not attain the political subjecthood of 'grievable lives.' Apart from attaining a bureaucratic label and some material compensation, justice still remains impotent when it comes to the balance between lives lost, life worlds transformed on one side and perpetrators named through a system of justice on the other. Perhaps this is the reason why the narration of the widows' lives always starts with the point at which their relationship with 'normal life' breaks. Every moment of the past, the present and future evolves out of the infinite event of transformation. Had there been any formal closure achieved, there might have been the possibility of a different temporal bracketing to the narration.

Not only is there an exile of these lives from the 'normal' unfolding of personal biography, there is a corporeal crystallization to this, precisely because these are lives led in relation to other cityspaces. In other words there is an actual address of exile which the widows inhabit. By founding a colony for widows of the 1984 riots, it was as if bureaucratic injunction, by demarcating a spatial limit to a place had not only 'produced' a space of victimhood, but also, with the same stroke, ascribed a possible destiny of exclusion to its residents. A recent newspaper report[29] suggests a similar zoning adopted, by 'choice' and not by formal rule, by riot victims of the post-Godhra violence in certain Gujarat villages, echoing patterns already prevalent in Surat and Ahmedabad. Instead of returning to their original homes, most of these people are choosing to relocate themselves in areas they deem safer, thus Muslims are choosing 'safety in numbers' by moving to predominantly Muslim villages, as the report suggests. One of the reasons cited for this is the victims' continued involvement in court cases so long as some of the neighbors continue to figure in the names of the accused, the returnees are unlikely to find much peace or personal security.

---

[28] Ibid.
[29] Indian Express. March 6th 2005. Reporter, Milind Ghatwai

Although the instances do not necessarily need be read as comparable, a pattern takes form, one that is most likely to crystallize into long durations in the spatial future of the city. It is the mapping of an urban topography by which identifiable, recognizable groups of people who are most likely to be unsuccessful in shedding their label are 'allotted' their designated space in the density of the city, in other words, the *emplacement* of victims. The colony thus becomes a place with a label, a label that pre-empts biographical trajectories of its inhabitants with a sign that works both as a private mark as well as a public burden. Although, at first glance, the topography of the area would suggest nothing different from other similar colonies around the city, there is an important difference. It is as if the event of '84 has constructed, brick by brick, in these people's lives, perhaps even sustained by the outside world, a veritable wall that insulates the community within. On one hand, it is a circumscribed geography of mourning. One of our informants who was a very young widow in '84 had spent the last twenty years in the colony and was also successful in putting together a reasonable life for her family (the children were educated, one had a job), said when I asked whether she ever thought of leaving the colony to a better place, "Here I can talk everyday about '84. I can share my burden everyday. But anywhere else, people will just be tired of me; the mad woman who only talks about one thing."[30]

---

[30] One reading of this kind of repetition could be what Dori Laub M.D. "An Event Without a Witness: Truth, Testimony and Survival," in Shoshana Felman and Dori Laub (eds.) *Testimony: Crises of Witnessing in Literature, Psychoanalysis, and History* (New York: Routledge, 1992) writes with reference to her recording of Holocaust testimonies, "Trauma survivors live not with memories of the past, but with an event that could not and did not proceed through to its completion, has no ending, attained no closure, and therefore, as far as its survivors are concerned, continues into the present and is current in every respect. ...To undo this entrapment is a fate that cannot be known, cannot be told, but can only be repeated, a therapeutic process – a process of reconstructing a narrative, of reconstructing a history and essentially, of *re-externalizing the event* – has to be set in motion. This re-externalization of the event can occur...only when one can articulate and *transmit* the story, literally transfer it to another outside oneself and take it back again, inside." Laub, "An Event Without A Witness...," 69. Perhaps, the geographical proximity of a community of victims provides for this kind of therapeutic externalization and then internalization here, in a profound act of mutuality. This aspect ties in also with the kind of temporal bracketing mentioned earlier.

On the other hand, it is a bounded locale of social crisis. Most of the widows who had initially formed the small community of residents here came in with their remaining family members either very young children or elderly relatives.[31] As mentioned earlier, soon after their relocation to the colony, almost all the widows had to leave their homes to eke out a living. Some availed the sewing work provided by Nishkam that required them to work at a designated sewing center nearby. Others had to travel further away for jobs that were provided in government offices. The children had to fend for themselves or, more appropriately, as we were told by some of our informants, grew up free from the supervision of any male guardian. Naturally, we were told, these children, particularly the boys grew up to fall prey to the predictable evils of poverty and deprivation such as, drug abuse and petty crimes. Drug related deaths in the Colony were considered very high – about 200, possibly an exaggerated number, in the first half of 2004 alone.

This deprivation of proper, meaning 'male,' parenting had allegedly created a whole generation of misguided young men, which led to the whole colony acquiring a bad name. Some of the younger informants we talked to told us how their efforts at looking for jobs were routinely thwarted. One of them told us the story of a friend:

> A: A friend of ours had learnt the work of air conditioners. He went to an interview and everything was fine. At the end they asked him, where do you stay? And he said. Tilak Vihar. They said you have to go, we cannot take you. Because you are from Tilak Vihar. Just because of this word. They say, everybody is aberrant here, we are disreputable. Someone is a pickpocket, someone is a thief – you catch them and they say they are from Tilak Vihar.
>
> … They say you are from '84. There is such dirt there (in the colony), you must also be doing the same. We can only say

---

[31] In our current fieldwork we came across some male members in certain household who did not belong to the category of fathers or sons. Their relationship to the 'widow' was hard to establish, at any rate this was not information that was easily forthcoming. We sensed that it would be very detrimental to broach the topic of remarriage – nonetheless, if pursued it could have lead to a further analysis on how the constructed nature of this community of widows influences the engagement with the usual social sanctions and taboos of widowhood.

that five fingers are not the same. If along with four bad ones here there is another, he will also be considered bad.
C: Shahpura is even worse than Tilak Vihar. All bad things happen there – chain snatching, kidnapping, but only Tilak Vihar is considered disreputable.

Moreover, a whole colony composed mostly of young widows and their potential sexual availability could not have remained long from speculation. Remarks came our way from the younger informants about how the local police, in small everyday incidents refer to the women in very abusive language. The women also told us about their early years when neighbors close to the colony considered them to be potentially 'bad' women. Like some other poorer localities of the city, this Colony could also have been explained away by the various factors of urban deprivation. But this is a special colony, rendered so not only by its inmates but also by a society outside, both of which negotiate the place as one saturated with more meaning than poverty can bestow, it is a society of victimhood that has moved in time into a grievance of entitlement because of violence, of loss that bizarrely creates an milieu that combines a relentless but impotent public consciousness with the sharpness of continued private agony.

In a sense, a converse reflection of Poussin's painting could perhaps be possible if and when the city/state brings the survivor back into its fold. Only, when their past has been given due presence in the history of the ordered city/state, can these lives liberate themselves from their temporal bond, from their suspension in an exile from the flow of ordinary time, so that their biographies achieve a sense of ordinariness.

Concluding Comments: The Future of Memory
In the period that has passed between then and now, in the era when lives were meant to be reclaimed, it seems that another future to these memories has been manifested. It is not as if these stories have not found a future, in fact, they have taken the form of

repetitive representation in public consciousness – cinema,[32] media, non-governmental or community archives, public debate etc. They have become a discursive motif with which to identify civil violence in independent India (very different from the Partition), to make visible the political and legal negligence in attributing accountability or justice. However, in the realm of private telling and listening, these stories appear as motifs of failed mourning, of unsuccessful grief, as persistent interruptions in biographies that are to be recuperated. The stigma of injustice and the agony of bad fate continue to hinder any process of healing. These are not memories of experience that give their subjects a status of noble suffering. Rather they seem to overwhelm the project of continued life with the spreading decay of deprivation and victimhood.

Twenty years since entitlements and compensations have were allotted and dealt with, life in the Colony has continued in hues composed by both an irremovable stain of a past event and the newer tones of a relentless everyday life of new generations and transformed lives. In such futures of memories of violence, what is the modality of recovery? The notion of recovery in the social anthropological grasp of lives after violent devastation has been hinged on the reclamation of the everyday, on regaining normalcy.[33] It is the idea of normalcy and everydayness that intrigues and complicates the idea of recovery in the Colony.

In the ethnographic depiction of life in the Colony, normalcy should be defined within its contextual limits. There is perhaps nothing extra-normal in the bare daily running of these households. The routine and rhythm of life goes on, even beyond the everyday to emerging life stories. Just as an everydayness goes on with people going to work, with children going to school or staying behind, with household chores being attended to, other ordinary events of daughters and sons getting married, someone dying or being born, some-

---

[32] "Kaya Taran" and "Amu" are feature films made in the last two years, both of which portray stories whose protagonists' lives are woven through by the Sikh Riots of Delhi.

[33] See Veena Das, Arthur Kleinman, Margaret Locke, and Mamphela Ramphele (eds.) *Remaking a World: Violence, Social Suffering and Recovery.* (Berkeley: University of California Press, 2001). The authors list a few notions by which to approach the ethnographies and analysis of social suffering and recovery, amongst which is the idea of a return to the everyday.

one finding or losing a job go on. However fleeting the sense of the everyday, there is a stable sense of ordinary life that goes on amongst the widows, their families and their neighbors. In so far that normalcy is the reclamation of the everyday, it is there.

At the same time, we were also told repeatedly that not a day goes by when 1984 is not mentioned. I would argue that this is a normalcy, in its essence, engendered and then sustained by a moment of transformation. This moment, in the biographies of these women is the event of the riot. While a particular material side to life, a house, for some a source of income occasional or regular, a few other 'goods' and expenses have accumulated to standard of corporeal normalcy, these women lead a life anchored to a moment in their past which has made them conscious of a profound transformation. In Butler's words,

> ...one mourns when one accepts that by the loss one under-goes one will be changed, possibly for ever. Perhaps mourning has to do with agreeing to undergo a transformation (perhaps one should say *submitting* to a transformation) the full result of which one cannot know in advance. There is losing, as we know, but there is also the transformative effect of loss, and this latter cannot be charted or planned.[34]

The widows of 1984 lead transformed lives made acute by the fact that the perpetrators of the violence inflicted on them continue, in the eyes of their victims, their ostensibly unchanged lives. It is this acute contrast between two sides of normalcy – the ostensibly normal lives of the perpetrators who remain unaccountable and that of the widows whose apparently normal lives are led in constant futile mourning that makes their possible recovery to normalcy an irredeemable burden.

In the course of this essay, I have tried to show the various axes along which a survivor has to fragment in order to make ordinary life possible. Once marked by violence that remains unresolved, a certain trajectory of self-s seems to take course, on one hand in relationship to the city/state, and to public socialities on the other – as victims, as claimant, as a threat (to the transparency of statecraft, to

---

[34] Judith Butler, *Precarious Life*, 19 –49, discusses the transformative effect of grief.

the recovered community), as a stigma and as an unfulfilled grieving subject. It becomes schizophrenic terrain for the work of anthropology itself – how does one bridge the gap between lies and fact, its knowing and validation when it appears to be the same gap that sets up schisms between the institutions of state, the legal, the political and the executive just as it fragments public spheres, civil societies and communities.

Yasmeen Arif *is a Visiting Associate Fellow at the Center for the Study of Developing Societies, Delhi, India. Largely directed by an interest in complex urban conditions, her current research commitments include ethnographic and theoretical explorations of post – crisis urban situations and complex multi-community urban socialities. Her fieldwork experience, in this regard, has been in Beirut, Lebanon and in Delhi, India. She has also worked on issues relating to anthropology in history and its implications in a post–colonial, trans-national world. She has written both on recovery and reconstruction in post–war Beirut and on the making of world anthropologies.*

Religious Iconography, Violence, and Making of a Series

Mani Shekar Singh

Abstract
This paper analyses a series of compositions depicting the Gujarat violence of 2002 by Santosh Kumar Das, a Maithil artist from Ranti village in Madhubani district of Bihar. The analysis broadly reflects on whether a pictorial tradition such as Maithil painting, predominantly rooted in Hindu cosmology, has the capacity to depict contemporary violent political events like the one that unfolded in Gujarat. The compositions constituting the series, as the paper illustrates, resist the "eye-witness principle" so essential to the construction of history painting or the working of the "mediascape." Rather the artist narrates the event by temporalizing the different sections of the image-field in what are sometimes extremely complex and sophisticated techniques. Even when the "micro-themes" are derived from particular historical events, they are often placed within a mixture of other time frames and in the process constructing a hybrid pictorial space, a sort of montage that does not aspire to represent any phenomenological experience of what Nelson Goodman calls the reality made world. Taking recourse to imagery from Hindu mythology, and iconographic tradition of Maithil painting, the artist creates alternative formulations around motifs and icons to mount a powerful critique of the violence produced, and indeed celebrated by the Hindutva politics in the name of tradition.

In this paper,[1] I analyse a series of twenty-three compositions in *kachani* or line-drawing style of Maithil painting[2] by Santosh

---

[1] This paper is primarily based upon ethnographic interviews with Santosh Kumar Das, which I conducted in 2003 and 2004 in Ranti village of north Bihar in India. I am deeply grateful to Santosh for entrusting me with his stories, his memories, and his paintings. I am equally indebted to of the Ethnic Arts Foundation (EAF) for providing me with photographs of Santosh's Gujarat series. I have also benefited immensely from a community of scholars, in particular Veena Das, David Sanzton, Roma Chatterji, Deepak Mehta, Yasmeen Arif, and Pratiksha Baxi, with whom I have shared the life of a researcher. For their friendship and helpful suggestions, I am enduringly grateful.
[2] Maithil painting is traditionally a ceremonial art form performed on life cycle ceremonies (*samskara*), annual and weekly festivals (*puja*), and ritual vows (*vrata-*

Kumar Das on the 2002 violence in Gujarat and its aftermath.[3] The series, composed over a period of one year, is primarily based on stories and visuals that appeared in the print and electronic media after the Godhra train incident in February 2002. However, to construe from this that Santosh's pictorial rendering of Gujarat carnage is simply a replication of televisual and other mass media images would be to overlook the complexity of the series. The compositional structure of the Gujarat series, as I would like to illustrate, is not based on the "eye-witness principle," so essential to the working of what Arjun Appadurai[4] calls the "mediascape."[5] Neither is the series an attempt

---

puja) by women of Maithil Brahman and Karna Kayastha castes of Mithila, a geocultural space that coincides with the present day districts of north Bihar in India and the Nepalese *Terai*. All the other castes are said to follow their model. In literature on Maithil painting, a distinction is generally made between the "line-drawing" (*kachani*) style of the Kayastha painters and "colour-drawing" (*bharua*) style of the Brahman artists (see W. G. Archer, "Maithil Painting," Marg III [3], [1949], 29-33, and M.S. Singh, "A Journey into Pictorial Space: Poetics of Frame and Field in Maithil painting," *Contributions to Indian Sociology* [n.s.] 34 [3], [2000], 409-42). The Kayastha painters utilise the potentiality of line as a pictorial device for shading the required areas of figures and in the process convey some sense of volume. The term used to refer to the process of shading done with the help of firm but fine lines is *kachani*. This term, which comes close to incising, says a lot about the nature of the lines utilised in shading as well as the pictorial instruments. In contrast to the "line-drawing" style, most of the Brahman painters use colour as the pictorial means to rescue the figure from the flatness of the pictorial surface. The term generally used to refer to the coloured compositions is *bharua* or *bharnai* (literally meaning to fill in). The term *bharua* or *bharnai*, therefore, refers to the process of filling in colours within the limits defined by the outlines of figures. The compositions of the Brahman artists are more like coloured drawing rather than "painting" in the modern sense. With the commodification of Maithil art, these distinct traditions of pictorial practice have begun to overlap, thereby resulting in hybrid or "cross-over" styles (see M.S. Singh, *An Ethnographic Study of the Pictorial Traditions of the Dalits of Mithila*, Report submitted to India Foundations for the Arts, [Bangalore, 2003], and David Szanton, "From Village to World Market: Tradition and Modernity in Mithila Paintings," *Biblio*, [2004], 28-29).

[3] On the morning of 27th February 2002, at Godhra railway station a coach of the Ahmedabad-bound Sabarmati Express was set on fire along with fifty-eight helpless passengers. This led to a state-wide pogrom in which several hundred Muslims were ruthlessly massacred. See Siddharth Varadarajan, *Gujarat: The Making of a Tragedy* (New Delhi: Penguin, 2002), and Asghar Ali Engineer (ed.), *The Gujarat Carnage* (New Delhi: Orient Longman, 2003) for a detailed account on the Gujarat carnage.

[4] Arjun Appadurai, *Modernity at Large: Cultural Dimensions of Globalisation* (Delhi: Oxford University Press, 1997).

[5] The "eye-witness principle," as Ernst Gombrich informs us, is also valued in the genre of History painting. In composing such paintings the artist is not expected to include 'anything the eye-witness could not have seen from a particular point at a

to capture the "reality effect" of a medium communicating in the so-called real time, in the present.[6] Nor do the paintings work as "traces" of what Roland Barthes[7] famously described in the context of photographs as "this has been." Rather Santosh's Gujarat series of paintings operates between two world-views, between "myth" and "history." The series is deliberately "framed" by Hindu mythological stories (like the Ramayana) and icons. Such a framing, as it will become evident, enables Santosh to mobilize a powerful critique of *Hindutva* politics[8] from within traditions of Hinduism. Furthermore, by exceeding 'a single tense, one voice, and one time,'[9] the series is able to problematise the very notion of "facticity," which is said to frame the media images of our times.

The visuality which Santosh's Gujarat series makes available also raises a set of important questions about pictorial representations and their potentialities to convey truth. We are led to ponder whether a pictorial tradition like Maithil painting, which is predominantly rooted in Hindu cosmology, has the capacity to depict contemporary violent political events like the one that unfolded in Gujarat in 2002. Do the artists painting from within such traditions have the resources and pictorial techniques to meaningfully narrate events like the 2002 Gujarat violence in which several hundred Muslims were ruthlessly massacred? One of the aims of this paper would be to demonstrate how critique is mobilised by Santosh using painting's own properties and technical means, as well as iconographic resources of Maithil tradition.

---

particular moment' (Ernst Gombrich, *The Image & the Eye* [Oxford: Phaidon, 1982], 253).

[6] See Jacques Derrida and Bernard Stiegler, *Echographies of Television* (Cambridge: Polity Press, 2002).

[7] Roland Barthes, *Camera Lucida: Reflections on Photography* (London: Vintage, 1993).

[8] *Hindutva* is a key concept in Hindu fundamentalist ideologies, which dates back to the early twentieth century and to the notion of India as the nation of Hindus alone. At present, it is an ideology that exalts a certain version of the "religious, racial and cultural identity" of the Hindus as an assumed "majority community." Thus, *Hindutva* negates both the plural bases of Hinduism and democratic society.

[9] James C. Faris, "The Gaze of Western Humanism" in *The Anthropology of Media: A Reader*, Askew Kelley and Richard R. Wilk (eds.) (Oxford: Blackwell Publisher, 2002), 79.

Ganga Devi and the line-drawing tradition of Mithila

Santosh belongs to a family of well-known Kayastha painters from Mithila. After his initial training in Maithil painting, he went to Maharaja Sayajirao University, Baroda, in 1987 to pursue a course on Fine Arts. At Baroda, he was exposed to the nuances of modernist art and its compositional techniques. Ironically it was the works of Ganga Devi[10] and not those of the modernist painters that fuelled Santosh's pictorial imagination. On his return from Baroda in 1992, he decided to formally initiate himself in the "line-drawing" (*kachani*) tradition of Maithil painting through the works of Ganga Devi.[11]

There were two aspects of Ganga Devi's pictorial technique, which appealed to Santosh's aesthetic sensibility. 'If you look at her paintings,' Santosh informed me, 'Ganga Devi makes minimal use of colour, and all that is technically associated with the process of colouring (such as tonality, highlights, shading, etc.). She relies totally on the line to compose the pictorial space. This makes her technique relatively simple. But by the same token it also makes the act of painting (which is more like drawing) extremely challenging because every expression has to be achieved only through the resources of lines.' Santosh's own compositions, as I will point out, are unending experimentation with lines and their capacity to express form.

It would not be inappropriate to state that Santosh sees the Maithil pictorial tradition through the prism of Ganga Devi's compositions. Like Ekalavya, the archetypal pupil in Hindu mythology, he has accepted Ganga Devi as his teacher (although *in absentia*) and has worked towards mastering the technique of line-drawing by carefully studying her paintings. This period of learning, it must be pointed out, has also been a period of unlearning – i.e. of erasing his

---

[10] Ganga Devi is probably the most celebrated artist from Mithila. A vast majority of her paintings are about journeys to distant lands. These include series on the Ramayana epic, the life-cycle rituals, and journeys to Russia, the United States, Japan, etc. For a detailed study of her paintings see Jyotindra Jain, *Ganga Devi: Tradition and Expression in Mithila Painting* (Ahmedabad: Mapin, 1997).

[11] Santosh shut himself from the outside world for almost a decade after returning from Baroda. During this period he spent all his energy mastering what he refers to as 'the purity and stability of the line.' I have had the opportunity of seeing hundreds of his sketches from this period. The Gujarat series is one of the first major works done by him after returning from Baroda.

exposure to the academic art and its techniques of representation at the Baroda School. However, the process of learning and unlearning is never one of substitution. The Gujarat series of paintings makes it evident that his training at Baroda has facilitated his reworking of Maithil pictorial tradition in a particular way. It is clearly apparent in his deployment of series as a compositional device in the making of his paintings.[12] This is not to state that Maithil artists before him have not painted in series. Rather a large body of Ganga Devi's compositions are in the form of series.[13] Although Santosh has followed the tradition of working in series pioneered by Ganga Devi and a host of Maithil painters, a close analysis of his paintings immediately brings to our notice the fact that his deployment of series departs from the Maithil tradition in significant ways.

Unlike some of the other Maithil painters, his penchant for composing in a set of "transformative" repetitions as well as thematically related reflections on a set of themes is clearly influenced by the modernist tradition. As in the case of his Gujarat series, to which we will return later, repetitive rendering or variations provide a context of mutual elucidation for individual compositions. Such mutual elucidations, as Michael Fried[14] argues for some of the modernist painters like Noland and Stella, are both formal and expressive. Thus by presenting a number of compositions in the Gujarat series all of which essentially have the same approach to the same formal problem – for instance, how to depict bodies entrapped in flames without the resources of colour (see Fig. 5) – Santosh makes the representation much more accessible. Similarly the differences

---

[12] Besides the use of series as a compositional device, his exposure to academic art and its techniques of representation has facilitated his "play" with form, especially experimenting with anatomy of figures to convey certain moods (*bhava*), etc.

[13] She was probably one of the first Maithil artists to compose her paintings in terms of series. In one such series of autobiographical paintings, labelled as the "Cancer Series" Jyotindra Jain (*Ganga Devi*, 1997), she illustrates incidents such as her brother's death in the context of her own illness; her tedious journey from Madhubani to Delhi in torrential rain and floods; and her experience of painful treatment she received in the cancer wards of the All India Institute of Medical Sciences (AIIMS) in Delhi. The defining feature of the cancer ward series is repetitive rendering of her image in different sections of compositions constituting the series. Furthermore, each of the characters occupying the pictorial space with her is an identifiable person who has had an important role to play in her life.

[14] Michael Fried, *Three American Painters* (Harvard: Fogg Art Museum, 1965).

among the compositions within the series – for instance, people look-ing for safe shelters (see Figs. 10, 11 &12) – serve to cull out the par-ticular expressive intonation of each.

If his training at the Baroda School has facilitated his rework-ing of the Maithil pictorial tradition, then his explorations of the line-drawing or *kachani* tradition of Mithila has provided him an insight into the works of some of the modern masters like Picasso and Klee. 'When I was at Baroda,' Santosh confessed to me on a number of occasions, 'I couldn't comprehend the works of great painters introduced in the class by teachers. I couldn't understand the utilisation of form or colour by these artists in their paintings. It is only now, after I have spent years in mastering the line, that I under-stand what they are saying in their paintings.' His re-reading of Pi-casso is evident, as I will point out, in a number of his Gujarat paintings. It is also apparent in some of his more recent composi-tions.[15]

Images of gods as a framing device

Fig. 1

Santosh begins the series with a painting in which the mother earth is depicted shedding tears for the victims of the 2002 Gujarat violence (see Fig. 1). In the painting the circular image of weeping earth occupies the centre of the pictorial field. She is flanked by the

---

[15] A number of his paintings at once come to mind like the bulls entangled in a fight, lovers in a park, a man cycling down the road.

figures of Durga and Shiva, the primordial Hindu deities. Of the two, Durga is housed in the left[16] section of the pictorial field. She is shown in an upright posture, standing besides a tiger, her mount, facing the weeping earth. Her weapons are arranged around her in such a manner that they appear to be floating or suspended in air. In the painting, Shiva occupies the right section of the field. He is in *padma asana* (a setting posture with both the legs crossing each other), looking outward towards the spectator (see Fig. 1).

Fig. 2

The first painting in the series is based on a myth in *Devi Mahatmya*, which recounts the origin of goddess Durga. In the foundational myth, the gods after having suffered defeat at the hands of the demon king Mahisa approached Shiva and Vishnu for help. On hearing their plight, Shiva and Vishnu were enraged. Out of their rage was formed the goddess Durga. *Devi Mahatmya* then recounts how the goddess received her various limbs and weapons from different gods and how, thus constituted, she proceeded to vanquish Mahisa and his army. The myth ends with her consent to bring relief to those who will call upon her in future calamities.[17]

---

[16] Throughout this paper, I use the terms "left" and "right" to refer to the left and the right of the spectator of the painting. However, in many traditional art forms left and right always address to the left and the right of the image within the pictorial field. For a detailed analysis of the located properties of the pictorial field see Boris Uspensky, "'Left' and 'Right' in Icon Painting," *Semiotica* 13(1), (1975), 33-40.

[17] In his study of Goddess pilgrimage in the Himalayas, William S. Sax has explored how different regional traditions rework basic aspects of Devi's mythology in the light of local approaches to politics, social order, gender relations, and ritual practice

It is here that Santosh's composition plugs in. The earth mother weeps at the violence, which has unfolded in Gujarat. Shiva, who occupies the right section of the pictorial field, is infuriated at the unfolding of the events.[18] Once again he gives form to the goddess to defeat demonic forces (in this case led by Narendra Modi, the incumbent Chief Minister of Gujarat) and bring order. In the painting, the floating weapon around the image of Durga connotes this process, which is in motion. Throughout the series, as it will become evident, Santosh evokes myths and legends that juxtapose the righteous and the demonic forces, and the victory of the former over the latter.

As we shift our attention to the next composition in the series, we are faced with the figure of Ram as Vishnu's seventh incarnation in *abayadana mudra* (a gesture conveying tranquillity, compassion, and benevolence), occupying the central axis of the pictorial field (see Fig. 2).[19] As an icon, Ram is in direct visual contact with the spectators, engaging and returning their vision. The rest of the image-field is populated with figures of men, women, and sages paying homage to him. The iconographic details of Ram as *maryada purushottam*, the lord of the universe, make this composition stand out in the series. As already stated, Santosh provides the image of Ram a frontal posture, his right hand holds his bow and his palm faces the spectator showering blessings on them (see Fig. 2). The frontal image of Ram seeks the spectator so that s/he can obtain his *darsan* (a particular type of blessing conveyed through the eyes).

(William S. Sax, *Mountain Goddess: Gender and Politics in a Himalayan Pilgrimage* [New York: Oxford University Press, 1991]).

[18] Shiva has been depicted smiling in this composition. However, this must not be read as a depiction of Shiva as a god who smiles in the face of a cosmic tragedy. Rather, the depiction of smiling Shiva in this painting, which is typical to Maithil art, is expressive of his rage at the unfolding of the event.

[19] In this composition, the iconography of the figure of Ram needs to be noted. This depiction departs (or is distinct) from the image of aggressive, vengeful, muscular, and saffron-clad Ram (often towering above a new Ram temple in Ayodhya), which is propagated by the Hindu fundamentalist organisations like the *Vishwa Hindu Parishad* (the VHP), *Bajarang Dal*, and *Bharatiya Janta Party* (the BJP) (see Anuradha Kapur, "Deity to Crusader: The Changing Iconography of Ram" in *Hindus and Others: The Question of Identity in India Today* Gyanendra Pandey [ed.] [Delhi: Viking, 1993], 74-109). The image of Ram in Santosh's painting is in consonance with his visualization in Maithil tradition.

Fig. 3

The visualisation of Ram undergoes a subtle but definitive transformation in Santosh's third painting in the series. Here the figure of Ram is no longer an icon looming large over the spectator-devotee, demanding his/her attention. He, along with his brother Lakshman, is depicted paying homage to a *Shiva lingam* (a symbolic representation of Shiva) seated in a cave (see Fig. 3). 'This scene,' Santosh explained, 'is taken from the Ramayana. Ram and Lakshman prayed to Shiva so as to make their campaign against Ravana successful.' If the frontal image of Ram in the previous composition speaks to devotees and penetrates them with his intimate glance, then his profile face is detached and 'belongs with the body in action (or in an intransitive state) in a space shared with other profiles on the surface of the image.'[20]

The first three compositions, done using red and black lines, are overt depictions of Hindu deities. Why has Santosh thought it appropriate to begin a series on communal violence in this manner? How are we as spectators to comprehend these Hindu icons in the context of the 2002 Gujarat genocide? Furthermore, how does this group of compositions (Figs. 1, 2 &3) relate to each other and to the rest of paintings in the series? At this juncture, I would like to state that the problem, which the first set of compositions poses, especially with regard to their critical intent, begin to get resolved the moment we assess them in relation to the entire series of paintings. It would

---

[20] Meyer Schapiro, *Words, Script, and Pictures: Semiotics of Visual Language* (George Braziller, 1996), 73.

then become clear that these compositions are not isolated pictures and therefore cannot (or should not) be perceived individually. Through these initial compositions, which in a sense form a series (or a set) within the series, Santosh makes available to the spectators a religious iconography, which provides the semiotic infrastructure to the later figures in the series to make their intensities felt.[21] He makes it apparent that the 2002 events in Gujarat can be meaningfully grasped in relationship to the past, which lies outside linear historical time.

The burning train and the charred bodies

Fig. 4

---

[21] Religious imagery also forms an important part of a vast majority of chromolithographs and other visual fields produced in India during the colonial period. However, the use of such imagery as part of nationalist iconography, I feel, differs from the Gujarat series in determinate ways. During the colonial period, politics and religion were conceptually separated into distinct domains – politics being placed under strict surveillance and religion conceptualised as autonomous. The imposition of this distinction, as Christopher Pinney points out, had a paradoxical effect, 'for it encouraged the playing out of outlawed and fugitive political aspirations in the specially marked compartment of the "religious" constructed by romantic orientalists. This colonial space of the mythic was marked by a blindness, on the part of the colonists, to the power of the past in the present and the ways in which the past is continually remade' (Christopher Pinney, *Photos of the Gods. The Printed Image and Political Struggle in India* [Delhi: Oxford University Press, 2004], 640). The nationalist artists readily occupied this colonially sanctified mythic space to counter censorship and proscription. For Santosh, the use of allegorical visual signs and motifs is not so much about fighting a guerrilla war with the state and its practice of censorship. Rather it has to do with comprehension of the Gujarat event. For him the allegorical mode is the only way in which the Gujarat violent can be meaningfully narrated and comprehended.

The fatal tragedy at Godhra railway station on the 27th February 2002, which is said to have triggered the carnage, is the subject matter of the fourth painting in the series.

Santosh evokes this scene by depicting the train (Sabarmati Express) with its carriages engulfed by fire, burning to death fifty-eight passengers. Most of these passengers were voluntary workers (*kar sevaks*) returning home from Ayodhya, where they had gone to participate in a politico-religious ceremony aimed at forcibly constructing a Ram temple at the very site where the Babri Masjid once stood.[22] The manner in which Santosh depicts the engine of the ill-fated train within the pictorial space makes this painting compositionally distinct. The engine faces the spectator, thereby stressing its outward movement. Due to this compositional strategy, the train does not recede into the distant horizon; rather it proceeds toward the spectator (see Fig. 4). Thereby looming large on his/her consciousness, a constant reminder of the tragedy.

The next two compositions in the series are variations on the same scene – i.e. bodies trapped in flames. In both these compositions Santosh makes use of what one might call a "zoom-in" technique.[23] As a result, only the charred bodies in flames, devoid of any surrounding, are visible to the spectator (see Fig. 5). What also needs to be noted in both these compositions is the way in which flames take the shape of lotus petals. The two repeats make it evident that there is nothing incidental about this depiction. As spectators, we are led to ask whether there is any connection between death (the charred bodies), fire, and the lotus.[24] The fact that the bodies en-

---

[22] Ayodhya, a small pilgrim town in the Faizabad district of Uttar Pradesh, is said to be the birthplace of Ram. It is here that Babri Masjid, a sixteenth century mosque, was located before its demolition in 1992 by Hindu fundamentalist organizations. Over the last decade, the Babri Masjid-Ramjanmabhoomi controversy has been the main source of conflict between the Hindu and Muslim communities in India.

[23] The influence of film and its techniques of representation are evident in this composition and in the rest of the series.

[24] As *padmamula*, the lotus plant motif 'is the symbol of life originating from the germ in the dark primeval waters, and therefore Life out of Death' (J. E. Van Lohuizen, "Review of *The Golden Germ*," *Arts and Letters* XXVIII [1955], 59). Thus it occupies an important place in the Hindu cosmology. The lotus is also the national flower of India. Since it operates at these two registers (Hinduism and nationalism), it makes it into a very potent but a mobile symbol. By virtue of making the lotus its

trapped in fire were those of the *kar sevaks* or voluntary workers returning from Ayodhaya, most of whom were the *Vishwa Hindu Parishad* (henceforth the VHP)[25] and the *Bharatiya Janta Party* (henceforth the BJP)[26] supporters, gives the above correlation more credence.

Fig. 5

Both these compositions could also be seen as an experiment with a living landscape; an experiment in which the artist tests the capacity of different categories of being to invade and infest each other. At one level, this strategy builds on a pre-existing concern among Maithil artists with the capacity of visual forms to encompass the divine.[27] Santosh's experiments with the mutual imbrications of different domains are accented in radically different ways. His Gujarat series is a positive affirmation of a Maithil aesthetic in which figural excess signifies religious repleteness. In these two paintings, the image-signs work not through substitution but rather through addi-

---

party symbol, the BJP has successfully exploited its potency in the present political situation.

[25] The *Vishwa Hindu Parishad* (literally, "World Hindu Council") or the VHP was founded in 1964 to spread Hindu values and strengthen links among Hindus in India and abroad. The VHP's youth wing, the *Bajrang Dal* is particularly aggressive in its operational tactics and rhetoric.

[26] The *Bharatiya Janta Party* (literally, "Indian People's Party") or the BJP, founded in 1980, is a right-wing Hindu nationalist party. Although at the present the BJP occupies the seat of opposition in the Indian parliament, during the violence in 2002 it was heading the government at the centre and in the state of Gujarat.

[27] I am reminded here of Ganga Devi's paintings from her "Life cycle series" and the "Ramayana series" (see Jain, *Ganga Devi*, 1997).

tion – the flames remain flames but are then also revealed as lotus petals. Such compositions exemplify a crucial quality of the figural density as well as polysemic nature of Maithil imagery.

Trident and the lotus as symbols of aggression

Fig. 6

In the next composition, the pictorial field is divided into three vertical registers (see Fig. 6). The central register houses two of the most sacred symbols of Hinduism – i.e. the trident (*trisula*) and the lotus (*kamal*).[28] Within the pictorial space, these motifs also come to connote the BJP as well as an extended "family" of affiliated Hindu organisations under the leadership of the *Rashtriya Swayam-*

---

[28] As already stated, the lotus as the archetypal "tree of life" has multiple connotations in the Hindu mythology (see F. D. K Bosch, *The Golden Germ* [The Hague: Mouton, 1960]). In contrast, the trident (*trisula*) is associated with Shiva, the lord of lords (*Mahadeva*). As Shiva's weapon, the trident signifies the destruction of evil but also the bestowal of grace because it severs the human soul from the endless cycle of reincarnation.

sewak Sangh (henceforth the RSS),[29] popularly referred to as *Sangh Parivar*. Thus the trident is not simply an accessory of Shiva, but a weapon in the hands of the *Bajrang Dal* (youth wing of the VHP) activists to strike the enemy. Similarly, the motif of lotus in flames is indicative of the tension generated by the activities of the BJP, the VHP, and other members of the *Sangh Parivar* during the Gujarat violence. The whirlwind effect is further enhanced by the black and red strips of paint, which constitute the background pattern. Within the pictorial space of this composition, the wavy colour strips are centrifugal in its movement, always drifting away, participating in the construction of meaning elsewhere. Santosh uses such a whirling pattern, as I will point out, at different junctures through out the series.

The register occupying the left section of the field houses a figure of a Muslim male. His identity is caricatured in his clothing and echoed by the mosque in the background. A similar strategy is used by Santosh to depict a Hindu male, who occupies the right section of the pictorial field with a temple in the background. Both these figures are depicted as moving in opposite directions, thereby conveying a feeling of discomfort and uncertainty between them. This feeling is also connoted by their postures and gestures. The Hindu figure, for instance, is drawn in such a way that both his feet are pointing in opposite directions (see Fig. 6). This peculiar posture, often employed in comics, gives the figure an undecided or confused appearance.

According to media reports, the events that unfolded in Gujarat after the Godhra incident saw the emergence of new icons with political patronage, indulging freely in death and destruction. One such story, which finds clear expression in one of Santosh's paintings, has to do with a Hindu rioter indulging in terror campaigns against Muslim children. In order to narrate this event, Santosh composes the pictorial field in which the figure of a demon-like Hindu rioter dominates his surroundings. This larger than life image is shown ex-

---

[29] The *Rashtriya Swayamsewak Sangh* (literally, "National Volunteer Corps") or the RSS, founded in 1925, provides ideological direction to the *Sangh Parivar* (the so-called family of right-wing Hindu organisations), and controls a grassroots cadre.

tending one of his hands towards a group of terrified children.[30] With his other hand he is guarding the weeping children he has assembled on a platform. The background treatment of the section occupied by the Hindu rioter is the same as that of the central register housing the burning lotus and the trident in the previous composition. A similarity in whirling design composed of red and black strips at once enables the spectator to connect the two sets of images.

Fig. 7

By the time we come to the next composition, the man indulging in violence gains an iconic status. The statue-like figure is provided multiple outlines with the whirling pattern as the background (see Fig. 7). The multiple outlines produce a "stroboscopic effect,"[31] which animate the body. As a result of such a visual impact, the figure appears to be brandishing his sword from one hand to the

---

[30] See International Initiative for Justice Report, *Threatened Existence: A Feminist Analysis of the Genocide in Gujarat* (Bombay: New Age Printing Press, 2003) (henceforth IIJ Report) for the trauma on children in the aftermath of the Gujarat violence.

[31] Rudolf Arnheim, *Art and Visual Perception* (Berkeley and Los Angeles: University of California Press, 1954).

other.[32] Multiple outlines have often been interpreted as standing for a plurality of people. In this way, a single image can be made to stand for a crowd. This strategy, as Boris Uspensky[33] points out, is often utilised in folklore. The rest of the field is filled with tridents.

Fig. 8

In constituting the series, Santosh readily makes use of the same principles, which Sergei Eisenstein formulated as being essential to the construction of montage.[34] Within such a compositional organisation, as some of the paintings in the series illuminate, the coming together of images has the potentiality of generating a semantic charge, which neither image, taken in isolation, possesses, thus gen-

---

[32] A similar strategy is utilised by the Futurists and Cubists 'who tried to render motion through the multiplication of figures or parts of figures' (Arnheim, *Art and Visual Perception*, 412). One also finds such a compositional technique being used in comic art.

[33] Boris Uspensky, *A Poetics of Composition* (Berkley: University of California Press, 1973).

[34] In a montage, Ivavov argues, the coming together of two iconic signs in a syntagmatic sequence, gives rise to a complex abstract symbol that correlates with a new concept rather than with the denotate of the iconic signs combined (V.V. Ivanov, "Eisenstein's Montage of Hieroglyphic Signs" in *On Signs*, Marshall Blonsky [ed.] [Oxford: Basil Blackwell, 1985], 233).

erating what Roland Barthes[35] would call "obtuse meaning" from within.

The pictorial field of the next painting is divided into two horizontal sections. The upper section houses the colossal figure of Narendra Modi in profile with folded hands, looking away from the viewer (see Fig. 8). The burning background, teeming with figures with daggers in their hands, accentuates the image of Modi. The icon-like Modi is juxtaposed with the figure of Mahatma Gandhi, a forgotten man in his own land (see Fig. 8). The Mahatma is shown lying in his grave with "*Hey Ram*" (literally, "O Ram") inscribed on it in *Devanagri* (see Fig. 8). These are said to be the last words uttered by the Mahatma before his death at the hands of Nathu Ram Godse, a Hindu fanatic. The inscription "*Hey Ram*" is epigraphic in the classical sense. When read by the spectator, the inscription gives voice to the event that ensued in Gandhi's death. And thereby it assists in anchoring the floating chain of signifiers. The two sections, housing Modi and Gandhi, are joined by two rows of figures marching in unison from the left to the right of the field. These figures, which are flanked by the structures of a temple and a mosque, represent a section of Gujarati society trying to make sense of the situation.

The growing resentment against Modi's involvement in the carnage of innocent Muslims during the riots forms the subject of the next painting (see Fig. 9). The demand for Modi's removal as the Chief Minister of Gujarat can be read on a banner displaying the slogan "*Modi ko hatao*" in *Devanagri* (literally, "Remove Modi") in the lower section of the field (see Fig. 9). The background of this painting is a repeated pattern made of raised fists. Against this fist-pattern, signifying widespread protests, Santosh foregrounds a black figure in dancing posture with a sword in hand, probably representing *kaliyug* (the present degenerate epoch). The visual impact of this black dancing figure in the upper section of the composition is such that it submerges the protesters. This composition, therefore, brings to our notice that even with growing protest the dance of death continues. Given the subject of this painting it is not surprising to find that Santosh only makes use of black in composing the figures.

[35] Roland Barthes, *The Responsibility of Forms* (Oxford: Basil Blackwell, 1986).

Fig. 9

Safe shelters and relief camps

The next chunk of paintings in the series dwells on the micro-theme of safe shelters and relief camps[36] during and after the violence. In one of these paintings, three Muslim men, who can be identified by their attire, are shown rushing toward a safe hideout to escape the violent mob (see Fig. 10). Ironically these men are without

---

[36] During the Gujarat violence, thousands of Muslim families were compelled to flee their homes by violent mobs. Since these campaigns were led by the BJP and the VHP activists, the state government took absolutely no responsibility to provide these displaced families any safe shelters. As a result, the IIJ Report on Gujarat genocide narrates, 'the crucial responsibility of relief and rehabilitation were left for the most part to NGOs, many of them run by members of the Muslim community who were themselves affected by the violence. Many camps and temporary shelters were set up by these NGOs either in Muslim dominated areas or in towns where attacks were less probable – in graveyards, mosques, religious schools and open spaces in Muslim neighbourhoods' (IIJ Report, *Threatened Existence*, 54). The Report further informs us that 'a large majority of Muslims without alternative refuge stayed in these relief camps under terrible conditions from March to July 2002. ... The forcible closure of relief camps became politically expedient in order to erase visible wounds of the carnage. Gradual closures began from early April and finally, by mid July 2002, 11 of the 22 remaining camps were closed, once again displacing people without ensuing conditions for their safe return or rehabilitation' (IIJ Report, *Threatened Existence*, 55).

legs, which create a visual tension within the pictorial field. This is further heightened by the typical gesture of praying for safety. Despite the helpless condition of the men, indexed by their postures and gestures, the shelter turns hostile. This is represented by Santosh in the form of a large opening with sharp teeth-like inner lining (see Fig. 10). We often come across such imageries in *Puranic*[37] narrations in which demons are shown tricking men and gods through transfiguration – cave (as a shelter) transforming into a demon's mouth.

Fig. 10

In another variation on the theme of safe shelter, Santosh depicts a Gujarati Hindu family in typical Kathiawari[38] attire rushing towards a torch-shaped tunnel to escape the violence. The black background punctuated with tridents is indicative of the mood (*bhava*) of the prevailing situation – i.e. of despair and destruction. This particular painting reminds the spectator that the Gujarat violence had also impacted those Hindu families who had come to the rescue of their Muslim neighbours.

---

[37] As part of the *smriti* (non-Vedic scriptures), *Puranas* are a class of Sanskrit texts, which are devoted to the praise and glorification of deities.
[38] Kathiawara is a region in the Indian state of Gujarat.

The *Shah Alam* camp in Ahmedabad, which was one of the largest community shelters for Muslim families during and after the riots, constitutes the subject matter of two paintings in the series. In the first version, the upper section of the pictorial field is filled with two rows of faces looking in opposite directions (see Fig. 11). The lower section is occupied by figures of two women in a sitting posture with a child in their laps. A leafy plant emerging from the base proliferates to cover the background. In the process, it binds the different sections of the pictorial field (see Fig. 11). In this composition, Santosh has used the plant and children as motifs representing hope and regeneration amidst the dark despair of genocidal violence that sought to exterminate the entire Muslim community.

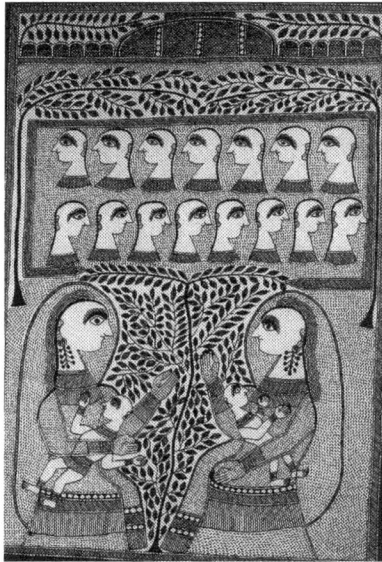
Fig. 11

As we shift to the next version of the *Shah Alam* camp theme, there is significant alteration in the pictorial structure. We are presented with a much gloomier picture of the riot situation (see Fig. 12). In the upper section the bust-like figures are confined within small black squares; thus conveying a sense of anxiety and fear. In the lower section, the seated women of the previous composition (see Fig. 11) gives way to figures of women in a standing posture, with one of their hands supporting their chins (see Fig. 12). This gesture imparts a worried look to the figures. Similarly the leafy plant of the previous composition matures or transforms into a tree with lots of flowers in this painting, but against a black background. The *Shah Alam* compositions bring to our notice that the repetitive rendering of a theme, which marks alteration of pictorial field, signifies related transformations of syntax in the interest of saying something new.

Fig. 12

The penultimate painting of the series is a telling comment on the nature of medical relief provided to the survivors in hospitals and the camps. There is a great deal of evidence that establishes the complicit role of state hospitals officials and health professionals in preventing the injured during the violence from accessing medical care. In the painting (see Fig. 13), Hanuman, the monkey lieutenant of Ram, is shown gliding through patches of clouds balancing a mountain on his palm bearing the inscription AIIMS (All India Institute of Medical Science, New Delhi). Santosh spoke about this painting as being 'a sequel to the Hanuman legend from Ramayana.' In Ramayana, Hanuman is said to have brought the entire mountain full of *sanjivani buti* (a life-saving herb) to the battlefield so that Lakshman could be treated with it. In this painting, the oral/written scene from Ramayana undergoes a visual substitution: the *sanjivani buti* is substituted by AIIMS, battlefield by relief camps, and Lakshman by ailing Muslim families. A full semantic unravelling of the picture depends not only on the spectator's knowledge of the Ramayana scene, but also on her/his familiarity with the image of Hanuman carrying the mountain with *sangivani buti* to save the life of Lakshman. Only then the spectator will be able replace *sangivani buti* with AIIMS, which Hanuman on Ram's order brings in order to save the lives of people in relief camps.

The Gujarat series concludes with a painting in which Santosh brings together distinct but interconnected micro-themes (see Fig. 14). In the lower section, framed figures of Ram and Gandhi are mounted on top of a burning train. Both these figures are in standing posture, looking away from the spectator. They are shown shedding tears with one of their hands on their foreheads, a gesture signifying pain and anguish. Together these grieving figures of Ram and Gandhi represent for Santosh that face of tradition, which has been made redundant by *Hindutva* politics.

The helplessness of Ram and Gandhi in the painting is made more pronounced by a large black trident piercing the image of weeping mother earth (see Fig. 14). The image of earth in distress due to the scar left by the trident (violence enacted in the name of religion during the carnage), links this composition to the first in the series (see Fig. 1). Thereby establishing, to use Umberto Eco's terms,[39] 'syntagmatic concatenations,' which greatly enhances 'argumentative capacity' of the motifs. Repetitive rendering of motifs (and background treatment), as I have tried to point out, not only links different paintings in the series, but also curbs what Christopher Pinney in the context of calendar prints calls 'the "figural" ambiguity and unruliness of a single image'[40] by positioning it within sequences of other images or motifs. It is the concatenation that reduces ambiguity.

---

[39] Umberto Eco, "Critique of the Image" in *Thinking Photography*, V. Burgin (ed.) (Basingstoke: Macmillan, 1982), 38.
[40] Christopher Pinney, "An Authentic Indian 'Kitsch'" *Social Analysis* 38, (1995), 100.

Fig. 13

Throughout the series, Santosh makes strategic use of Hindu religious symbols, motifs and icons (such as the lotus, trident, and the *Shiva Linga*) as well as the relevant scenes from the Ramayana and other Hindu mythological texts. However, this strategy need not be read as an apology on the part of an artist located within Hindu tradition. Rather his compositions make it evident to the spectator that religious icons are historically mutable, multivalent, and open to political disputation and manipulation. In the *Sangh's* visualisation, Ram is seen as the primary metonym of Hindu India. 'Sri Ram,' Lal Krishna Adavani had pronounced in the 1993 BJP *White Paper*, 'is the unique symbol, the unequalled symbol of our oneness, or our integration, as well as of our aspiration to live the high values.'[41] However, Santosh's paintings convey to the spectator that the image of Ram, as part of Indian tradition and aesthetic sensibility, is more complex than the manner in which he is represented by the VHP and the BJP (or the *Sangh Parivar*). In the cultural landscape of Mithila, for instance, Ram is omnipresent not only as Vishnu's incarnation, but equally as *pahun* (son-in-law). He is worshipped all over Mithila

---

[41] Quoted in Richard H. Davis, "The Iconography of Rama's Chariot" in *Contesting the Nation. Religion, Community, and the Politics of Democracy in India*, David Ludden (ed.) (Philadelphia: University of Pennsylvania Press, 1996), 35.

as *maryada purushotam*, the lord of the universe. But he is also visu-alised as the husband of Sita, the archetypal daughter of Mithila. And it is as Sita or Vaidehi's husband that he is fondly remembered in scores of songs sung by Maithil women during the marriage cere-mony.[42] It is this cultural legacy that allows Santosh to contest the appropriation of the figure of Ram by the VHP and the BJP. From this vantage point, one can say that the entire Gujarat series is an interruption of the global homogenising discourse of *Hindutva* poli-tics of the VHP and the BJP (or the *Sangh Parivar*) by the local.

Fig. 14

The Gujarat series is a lament, an expression of grief articu-lated by the artist (using resources of his tradition) in the face of vio-lence unleashed by *Hindutva* politics. As the compositions in the series make it evident, not only humans but also Hindu gods and goddesses mourn the loss and destruction of the Muslim community in Gujarat. Thus in the very first composition of the series (see Fig. 1), we may recall, it is the images of weeping earth surrounded by deities, which occupy our attention. By making the gods into wit-

---

[42] The imagery of Ram has a very intimate association for the people of Mithila. This intimacy is conveyed both pictorially and through marriage songs (*geet*) during a marriage ceremony.

nesses as well as party to his lamentation, Santosh transforms the Gujarat riots of 2002 from a local or regional tragedy into a catastrophic event of cosmic proportion.[43] And in the process, he constitutes a community that transcends not only spatial localisation, but also linguistic and religious boundaries.

Although Santosh's compositions are not traditional (in the sense of ritual diagrams done on ceremonial occasions within domestic spaces), in mounting a powerful critique of the violence, it readily draws on resources that are part of Maithil tradition. In an important sense, the series has a Maithil signature. Taking recourse to popular mythological imageries, Santosh weaves a masterful tangle of allusions, hidden meaning, and allegory that traverse what Walter Benjamin termed "messianic time" and a "homogenous, empty time" or between cosmology and history. Thus contesting any sort of "linearization" that may be inherent in the construction of media images. He creates alternative formulations around motifs and icons whose meanings are always in deferral. As the sixteenth century poet Tulsidas reminds the reader in *Ramcharitmanas*, the glorious acts of Ram may always be sung in new ways. Ram himself might even reappear, as he does in Santosh's Gujarat series, not as a vengeful god – as often made explicit in *Ramjanmabhumi* posters produced and distributed by the VHP[44] – but as someone mourning (with other deities and Gandhi) the death and destruction of the Muslim community. 'Gods,' Santosh reminded me, 'can never be communal.'

As a hybrid pictorial space, the Gujarat series, one might say, exists within a wider visual culture in which there is a continual spillage through processes of "inter-ocularity"[45] between the idioms of popular mythological theatre, chromolithography, photography,

---

[43] This strategy of making the gods into witnesses of catastrophic events is not limited to the Gujarat series. In a series of sketches depicting the September 11 attack on the World Trade Centre in New York City, Santosh has shown the gods grieving the tragedy from their heavenly abode. Similarly, Baua Devi has expressed the event through her signature motif, the *naga* (snake-god). Two weeks before the attack on the WTC, she painted a *naga* that rose from the golden earth in divine splendour. On the 13th September she painted the same *naga*, but now embracing a world in black, and writhing against a flaming sky.

[44] See Kapur, "Deity to Crusader…"

[45] Arjun Appadurai and Carol A. Breckenridge, "Museums are good to think: Heritage on view in India" in *Museums and Communities*, I. Karp, S. Levine and C. M. Kreamer (eds.) (Washington, D.C.: Smithsonian Institution Press, 1992), 34-55.

television, film, and other visual medium. Such conversations between different media not only facilitate visual inter-referencing but
also encourage visual quotation. I have attempted to illustrate that
each painted line and motif executed in the Gujarat paintings is con-
sciously related by Santosh to the media images (which provide the
raw "data" for the series) as well as to other mythographic representations. But what also needs to be noted is that each of the painted
lines or strokes is also related in a very determinate way to every
grapheme[46] already inscribed on the surface. Thus the process of
painting is the end result of countless decisions on the part of the
painter, almost always mediated by a sense of history and tradition.

The Gujarat series of paintings, as I have attempted to illustrate in this article, is a complex articulation by a painter rooted in
his own tradition. Such rootedness need not necessarily mean a passive acceptance of tradition. When one inherits, one sorts, one sifts,
one reclaims, and in the process reactivates what one inherits. The
visuality that Santosh makes available through his paintings – a visuality that highlights pluralism of Hindu traditions using figurative
elements and colours that are typical to his aesthetic sensibility – expresses initiative; it expresses the signature or countersignature of a
critical selection. It goes without saying that the appeal of the compositions that constitute the series also lie in its Maithil *trait*,[47] as
well as in the virtuosity of its highly personal sense of history.

---

[46] I use the term *grapheme* to indicate written marks, strokes, incisions, or "painterly
traces," which are as much the product of the act of painting as they are of writing.
See Jacques Derrida, *Of Grammatology* (Maryland: The Johns Hopkins University
Press, 1976).
[47] The term has two primary senses: etymologically, it refers to a graphic line, or
more specifically, to the action of drawing a line or set of lines (a stroke, a draft, a
"touch" in a picture); by extension, it is also used to designate a distinguishing quality or characteristic mark, a feature that allows one to identify or recognise a thing.

LIST OF ILLUSTRATIONS

Fig. 1: Mother Earth (centre) weeping for the victims of the 2002 Gujarat violence, with Durga (left) and Shiva (right). Santosh Kumar Das. *Collection courtesy Ethnic Arts Foundation.*

Fig. 2: A frontal image of Ram (centre) being worshipped by the laity and sages. Santosh Kumar Das. *Collection courtesy Ethnic Arts Foundation.*

Fig. 3: Ram and Lakshman paying homage to *Shiva lingam* (symbolic representation of Lord Shiva) in a cave. Santosh Kumar Das. *Collection courtesy Ethnic Arts Foundation.*

Fig. 4: A scene depicting the Sabarmati Express in flames at Godhra railway station in Gujarat on February 27, 2002. Santosh Kumar Das. *Collection courtesy Ethnic Arts Foundation.*

Fig. 5: A scene depicting bodies entrapped in lotus shaped flames. Santosh Kumar Das. *Collection courtesy Ethnic Arts Foundation.*

Fig. 6: Muslim (left) and Hindu (right) figures, with mosque and temple in the background, bifurcated by trident (*trisula*) and burning lotus (*kamal*). Santosh Kumar Das. *Collection courtesy Ethnic Arts Foundation.*

Fig. 7: A Rioter brandishing sword. Santosh Kumar Das. *Collection courtesy Ethnic Arts Foundation.*

Fig. 8: A scene depicting Narendra Modi, the Chief Minister of Gujarat, acquiring iconic status with spread of violence. Mahatma Gandhi is shown receding into oblivion. Santosh Kumar Das. *Collection courtesy Ethnic Arts Foundation.*

Fig. 9: The political opponents of Narendra Modi, the Chief Minister of Gujarat, displaying a banner stating "Remove Modi." Santosh Kumar Das. *Collection courtesy Ethnic Arts Foundation.*

Fig. 10: Gujarati Muslim men seeking shelter from rioters. Santosh Kumar Das. *Collection courtesy Ethnic Arts Foundation.*

Fig. 11: Gujarati Muslim families finding shelter in *Shah Alam dargah.* Santosh Kumar Das. *Collection courtesy Ethnic Arts Foundation.*

Fig. 12: Gujarati Muslim families finding shelter in *Shah Alam dargah.* Santosh Kumar Das. *Collection courtesy Ethnic Arts Foundation.*

Fig. 13: Hanuman, the monkey lieutenant of Ram, carrying the All India Institute of Medical Sciences (AIIMS) to relief camps. Santosh Kumar Das. *Collection courtesy Ethnic Arts Foundation.*

Fig. 14: Ram and Gandhi mourning trident's piercing the earth. Santosh Kumar Das. *Collection courtesy Ethnic Arts Foundation.*

Mani Shekhar Singh *(shekharmani@yahoo.com) is a Rockefeller Fellow at the Department of Anthropology at the Johns Hopkins University, Baltimore. He is currently engaged in research on the Pictorial Practices of Dusadh Children in Bihar (India). His publications include articles in Contribution to Indian Sociology (ns), Economic and Political Weekly, and Indian Folklife. His areas of research interest include visual anthropology, folk painting, political cartoons and posters, and child art.*

Adjudicating the Riot:
Communal Violence, Crowds and Public Tranquillity in India

Pratiksha Baxi

ABSTRACT
This paper looks at the construction of the communal riot in juridical discourse in India. Based on an analysis of appellate judgments, the paper looks at how the judicial discourse on riots regulates, normalises and sanctions illegal state violence, while it ascribes the failure of law to assign responsibility to the very nature of the violence. As the inverse of the public, the image of the crowd is deployed to deny the role of the state through acts of commission or omission in the constitution of communal violence. Judicial discourse constitutes the violent crowd as a site of passion, while it feminises crowd violence by divesting the crowd of the underlying politics of masculinity. The absence of the testimony to sexual violence during communal violence in legal records has been used to distinguish the riot from genocide. The judicial pronouncements on communal harmony, in contrast, offer a reading of the way the potentialities of public testimony meet closure. This adjudication of the potential of violence offers a reading of how law creates the conditions of communal violence, while bringing specific body populations under the category of legal governance. Communal harmony is adjudicated by setting up equivalences between crowd violence and sanctioned illegal state violence. Thereby the juridical archive is oriented to a different notion of future as compared to the one embodied in the archives of independent enquiries that document the manifold injuries inflicted during communal violence.

Introduction
Following the anti-Sikh violence in 1984, the 1992-93 violence against the Muslims and the more recent violence unleashed against the Muslims in Gujarat in 2002, many activists, lawyers and academics have argued that the legal category of "riot" fails to address the techniques, forms and scale of violence deployed against

Domains 3:66-101 | Copyright © 2007 South Focus Press

entire communities. In the context of Gujarat 2002, it has been argued that the riot related laws fail abysmally to address genocidal
violence on Muslim men, women and children. The difficulties in
assigning collective responsibility and the lack of criminal prosecutions suggest the need to re-examine the judicial discourse on communal riots. However, the recent proposed "riot" law, as it has been
dubbed, continues to be framed within the juridical discourse on
communal violence.

This paper, based on appellate judgments,[1] draws on the way
the riot is pictured in judicial discourse, to detail how the power of
state law creates *Kafkaesque* testimonial conditions for survivors of
communal violence. I suggest that the judicial discourse on the "riot"
regulates, normalises and sanctions illegal state violence and specific
forms of communal violence. I argue that the judicial discourse on
communal riots is organised around at least six defining characteristics. First, the "riot" is discursively constituted in judicial discourse
through specific classificatory practices, which ascribe the *failure* of
law in the face of collective violence to the very *nature* of "mob" violence. Second, judicial discourse is inflected by the discourses of
blame that positions communities of survivors as provocateurs and
thereby, worthy of blame. Third, the judicial discourse on communal
riots represses the violence survivors face, by domesticating certain
forms of violence as typical to a riot and by denying other forms of
violence that characterise the communal riot. Fourth, the emphasis
on the "communal" aspect of collective violence places culpability
and responsibility on communities as if the communities are engaged
in an equal and reciprocal exchange of violence based on primordial
and timeless notions of hatred. Fifth, the construction of the com-

---

[1] This paper is based on an ongoing survey of appellate judgments that address
communal riots to bring together the different sites at which the "jurisprudence of
the riot" finds articulation. I am grateful to Maya Ratnam for helping me compile
appellate judgments pronounced by the Supreme Court and four High Courts (Delhi
and Haryana, Punjab, Bombay and Gujarat) from 1984 to 2002. The selective reading of the judgments herein is supplemented with a reading of the relevant enquiry
committee reports on the violence in 1984 in Delhi and in Bombay in 1992-3. The
idea of such a collation is to develop an understanding of judicial discourse as it
moves across different body populations, contexts and episodes of violence rather
than compile a statistical enumeration of the outcomes or effects drawn from such
case law. In this way, legal discourse is the site, par excellence, of biopolitics. This
will be developed in a later paper.

munal riot in judicial discourse describes the failure of the state to desist from or contain communal violence, while leaving unacknowledged the fact that the power of the state flows from sanctioning the use of illegal state violence during communal riots.[2] This realm of illegality, which "preserves" law, remains a spectre in appellate judgments of riots. Finally, I draw attention to how communal riot, defined as an offence against public tranquillity in the Indian Penal Code (IPC), is also named as an act of terror in extraordinary law.

The Diminished Responsibility of Crowds

The debate regarding whether crowds are marked by passions or rationality has animated scholars concerned with collective action, individual responsibility and collective violence.[3] Crowds have been characterised as sites of passion, occupying a position analogous to that of the primitive, feminine and the barbarian.[4] Individuals, engaged in collective action, during crowd violence have been understood to bear diminished responsibility for their actions, since the crowd owns its subjects in ways the latter cannot control. The crowd has been characterised as an inverse mirror image of the public characterised by reason. Typically then the crowd in colonial discourse on communal violence has been invested with passion, the riot seen as a product of the primordial hostility between Hindus and Muslims, and communal violence represented as an outcome of the eruption of temporary frenzy of bloodthirsty crowds.[5] Pandey has forcefully argued that the 'communal violence narrative cannot but be a history of the state.'[6] Not only is the communal riot seen as primarily a law and order problem, argues Pandey, but the local is

---

[2] See Veena Das (ed.), *Mirrors of Violence: Communities, Riots and Survivors in South Asia* (Delhi: Oxford University Press, 2000). Also see Patricia Tuitt, *Race, Law and Resistance* (London: The Glasshouse Press, 2004).

[3] See Gustave Le Bon, *The Crowd: A Study of the Popular Mind* (Atlanta: Cherokee, 1982). Also see Serge Muscovici, *The Age of the Crowd: A Historical Treatise of Mass Psychology* (Cambridge: Cambridge University Press, 1985).

[4] See Susanna Barrows, *Distorting Mirrors: Visions of the Crowd in late Nineteenth Century France* (New Haven: Yale University Press, 1981).

[5] Gyan Pandey, "The Colonial Construction of 'Communalism': British Writings on Banaras in the Nineteenth Century" in *Mirrors of Violence: Communities, Riots and Survivors in South Asia* Veena Das (ed.) (Delhi: Oxford University Press, 1990), 94-134.

[6] Ibid., 132.

also seen as incapable of transformation apart from the influence of the colonial state. He indicates how the colonial communal riot narrative continues to structure contemporary accounts of the communal riot. Appellate judgments on communal riots then furnish a privileged site that allows us to detail this language of the state where "mob fury" and "timeless" hostilities between communities finds repetition in the judicial writing of communal riots in independent India.

A perusal of appellate judgments indicates that contemporary judicial interpretation of communal violence locates the crowd as the site of irrational passion where ordinary citizens who uphold everyday notions of public sociality are transformed into satanic beasts. Typically, we find descriptions of "infuriated mobs," or "blood thirsty assailants" who are "blinded by communal frenzy" in appellate judgments on communal riots. Consider the following case concerning Lokeman Shah who was charged with the murder of a police officer during the communal riots in Calcutta on 18th March 1984. The State of West Bengal appealed for an enhancement of the sentence to extreme penalty. The Supreme Court held that the

> Appellants had neither any previous enmity to the victims nor even any acquaintance with them. It is admitted fact that they acted in a rage of fury blindfolded by communal frenzy. We are aware that in most of the communal riots the participants are by and large illiterate and indoctrinated people. When the literate leaders try to keep themselves away, without participating in the perpetration of crimes though, perhaps, some such persons would fan up the communal frenzy by their utterances in the minds of the ignorant poor people who in a deranged fury rush into the streets prowling for prey. It was an unfortunate plight of the people who are ignorant about the real sublime thoughts of religions that they threw themselves into the cauldron of communal delirium which was burning up to boiling point. That was a time when the minds of the rioters turned demented and no sensible thoughts would enter into them. The leaders and the society have not played their part to teach them that religions are not meant for killing fellow human beings. If ignorance had prompted people to take up cudgels in the name of religion for indulging in carnage or murders they are no doubt liable to be convicted and sentenced for the offence committed by

them. But we have great difficulty to treat such a case as rarest of the rare cases in which the alternative sentence of life imprisonment can unquestionably be foreclosed.[7]

The characterisation of diminished responsibility of individuals when acting in concert in a crowd is best exemplified in *Kishori v State of Delhi*[8] – a case that may be positioned as the case *par excellence* detailing appellate jurisprudence of the crowd in the context of communal violence in contemporary times. It is important to mention briefly that Kishori, a well-known figure being the local butcher, was identified as an assailant amongst others in the mob, in the violence against the Sikhs in Trilokpuri,[9] Delhi. Nearly fifteen years later when the Supreme Court of India heard the appeal against the death penalty awarded to him by the Delhi High Court, Kishori had been charged and convicted in seven cases by the trial court. He was acquitted in four cases on appeal; only three cases had met with conviction of which two were appealed in the Supreme Court. I look at the first case of appeal since it was to become a precedent for other cases relating to the violence in Delhi in 1984.[10]

---

[7] *Lokeman Shah v State of West Bengal* 2001 SOL Case No. 258, 2001.04 .11 at Para 25.

[8] *Kishori v State of Delhi* (1999) 1 SCC 148.

[9] Trilokpuri, a resettlement colony, was formed following forcible evictions of people residing in slums and unauthorised colonies in the inner city, during the emergency. According to Kishwar around four hundred Sikhs were killed in Trilokpuri [Madhu Kishwar, "Gangster Rule: The Massacre of the Sikhs" *Manushi* 25 (1984)]. The largest number of killings was reported from two residential blocks dominated by Labana Sikhs - who had migrated from Pakistan. Labana Sikhs are lower in the caste hierarchy.

[10] In *Manohar Lal alias Mannu v State (NCT) of Delhi* [(2000) 2 SCC 92], the SC mitigated the death sentence to life imprisonment citing *Kishori v State of Delhi* [(1999) 1 SCC 148] as a precedent. In this case, Harbai testified that mobs armed with iron rods attacked her four sons in their house on 2.11.84 in Trilokpuri. Subsequently her sons were dragged outside the house, doused with petrol and burnt alive in the presence of the parents – the aging and blind father was spared. The Court adds, 'so it was the fate of the unfortunate mother to see every one of her four sons transforming into a life-struggling inferno' [(2000) 2 SCC 92 at 94]. The Delhi High Court confirmed the death sentence awarded by the Session Courts. It said that the case fell in the "rarest of the rare case" since this was 'not an ordinary routine case of murder, looting or burning. Members of a particular community were targeted, their properties looted and burnt and people done to death. The law and order machinery had completely broken down.... The situation created by the anti-communal forces cannot be viewed lightly and needs to be dealt with sternly. The after-effects of the

We learn from the Supreme Court judgment that Inder Singh, Sajjan Singh and Hoshiar Singh were murdered by a mob which included Kishori on the night of first November 1984. Asuadi Kaur wife of Inder Singh testified that mob entered their house. Her husband was attacked with a knife on his stomach, his hands cut off and the mob subsequently put a quilt on his body and burnt him. Other Sikh men hiding in the house were killed similarly. Asaudi Kaur testified that she was pushed out of the house at the time her husband was set on fire by the mob. She identified Kishori as a member of the mob, stating that her husband appealed to their friendship, and the fact that Kishori had a weapon in his hand. Likewise, Burfi Kaur, wife of Hoshiar Singh testified that her husband was killed by the mob, beaten with wooden sticks and killed due to repeated stabbing. However, Burfi Kaur – declared hostile by the prosecution - was not able to identify the accused. Bhakti Bai testified that her husband was attacked with a knife and when the mob realised that he was still alive, they set him on fire. Bhakti Bai was able to identify Kishori as a member of the mob that killed her husband in court.

The trial court was of the view that Kishori 'deserves death sentence as he has been convicted for murders for the seventh time and he had killed an innumerable number of Sikhs in a brutal manner.'[11] The Delhi High Court upheld the death penalty sentence on the grounds that 'the acts attributed to the appellant affect the basic feature of our Constitution, viz, secularism,'[12] and 'that the appellant indulged in riots resulting in killing of innocent persons, looting and burning their properties' – violence that 'would send shivers to any person.'[13] The Supreme Court however held that it was not found that Kishori was the leader of the mob or that he exhorted the others

---

incidents would be felt by the people left behind for years' [(2000) 2 SCC 92 at 95]. The Delhi High Court noted that the 'even though time is the best healer, certain situations cannot be retrieved or healed' in the case of the twenty seven year old pregnant wife of one of the slain men, or his mother who lost all her four sons [(2000) 2 SCC 92 at 95]. The Supreme Court mitigated the sentence on the grounds of diminished responsibility flowing from mob frenzy.

[11] (1999) 1 SCC 148 at 156.

[12] The extraordinary conflation between constitutional law and penal discourse may be noted here. The reference to constitutional transgressions is transferred hereinto the languages of everyday crime and punishment.

[13] (1999) 1 SCC 148 at 156.

to do any act. Nor did the courts of appeal uphold all the seven convictions. Moreover, the Supreme Court held that:

> In the present case, the prosecution case as unfolded before the Court, indicates that the riot in Delhi broke out as a result of the death of Smt. Gandhi and her death appears to be the symbol or the web around which the violent emotions were released. The death of Smt. Gandhi became a powerful symbolic image as a result of which the crowds were perpetrating violence in the height of frenzy. It is common experience that when people congregate in crowds, normal defences are lowered so that the crowd instinct assaults on the sense of individuality or transcends one's individual boundaries by offering a release of which the crowds were perpetuating violence in the height of frenzy. It is common experience that when people congregate in crowds, normal defences are lowered so that the crowd instinct assaults on the sense of individuality or transcends one's individual boundaries by offering a release [this kind of reiteration is typical in the writing of judgments] from inhibitions from personal doubts and anxiety. In such a situation, one can well imagine that a member of such a group loses one's self and the normal standard or sense of judgment and reality. The primary motivational factor in the assembly of a violent mob may result in the murder of several persons. Experts in criminology often express that when there is a collective action, as in the case of a mob, there is a diminished individual responsibility unless there are special circumstances to indicate that a particular individual had acted with any predetermination such as by use of weapon not normally found. If, however, a member of such a crowd picks up an article or a weapon which is close by and joins the mob, either on his own volition or at the instigation of the mob responding to the exhortation of the mob, playing no leadership, we may well say that such a person did not intend to commit all the acts which a mob would commit left to himself, but did so under the influence of collective fury.[14]

The standard of diminished responsibility then holds that the *nature* of mob violence provides a valid ground for mitigating the

---

[14] (1999) 1 SCC 148 at 155.

sentence.[15] This representation of the violent mob ignores the fact that 'if the community has a repertoire for the organisation of collective action, then so does the state for the management of these collective actions.'[16] Nor does this characterisation recognise that 'networks of people and relationships have to be mobilized in the creation of crowds,' since 'crowds are not built out of passive pools of people.'[17] Likewise, there is no contradiction between investing crowds with passion while bringing forth evidence of the organised nature of crowds since 'on the one hand, mob violence may be highly organized and crowds be provided with such instruments as voter's lists or combustible powders, and on the other that crowds draw upon repositories of unconscious images.'[18]

The split between crowds that are consumed by passion and crowds that work with a rationality finds elaboration in the Ranganath Misra Commission [RMC], a commission headed by Justice Ranganath Misra instituted to enquire into whether the 1984 riots in Delhi, Bokaro and Kanpur were organised, and whether the ruling party Congress-I was responsible for organising the riots. The Commission held that:

> The riots at the initial stage were spontaneous and by way of reaction to the situation but later the riots developed into a set type. The change in the pattern from spontaneous reac-

---

[15] The doctrine of "grave and sudden provocation" has been elaborated at length in Indian case law especially in the instance when husbands loose their self control when confronted with the *immorality* of their wives [or proof of their adultery], and anger drives them to murder their wives and/or their lovers. In *K. M. Nanavati* (AIR 1962 SC 605), the Supreme Court had held that the fatal blow should flow unambiguously from the provocation. If there was evidence, that time had lapsed between the provocation and the murder allowing the passion to cool, premeditation and calculation rather than provocation would be the legal standard to adjudicate the act as murder rather than manslaughter. In contrast, when we look at *Kishori v State of Delhi*, we find that the fact that the mob carried on killing over a day does put into question the temporary nature of mob frenzy. Indeed, we may ask how long does the temporary frenzy of the mob last. A comparative study of how judicial discourse constitutes passion across different juridical domains perhaps will provide different insights into the legal construction of the mob.

[16] Veena Das, *Mirrors*, 20.

[17] Veena Das, *Mirrors*, 28.

[18] Veena Das, *Mirrors*, 28.

tion to organised riots was the outcome of the take-over of
the command of the situation by anti-social elements.[19]

It is significant that when the spontaneous outburst of violence is seen as organised, directed and enacted at a later stage, it
congeals in the figure of the anti-social elements (and some lower
workers of the Congress). The anti-social element is contrasted with
the mobs that formed through collective passions spontaneously in
reaction to the assassination of Indira Gandhi and act to divest the
latter of a communal intent. These anti-social elements are typically
characterised as working class men stricken by envy of the rich,
heightened by the proximity of rich and poor in the urbanised Delhi.
We learn that rapid urbanisation has led to the rich and poor living
in close proximity bringing a 'sense of frustration' in the poor section
and 'a sense of hatred as also a lust for the property of the well to
do.'[20] Even though RMC finds that some middle class men were also
engaged in the violence and looting, mainly the violence is seen as the
handiwork of gleeful and jubilant anti-social men. We find that RMC
pictures an influx of anti-social elements from outside Delhi, who
travel on trains looting and killing Sikhs while the railway police
look on indifferently. We are told that the anti-social belongs to
Hindu and other non-Sikh faiths. I quote:

> The fact that local Hindus protected the Sikh residents as
> also their Gurudwaras from the onslaught of the riotous
> mobs in some areas is indicative of the fact that Hindus as
> such were not out to damage properties or make an attack on
> the lives of the Sikhs. It would, therefore, not be correct to
> say Hindus as a community carried the attack against the
> Sikhs, their properties and their places of worship...It is,
> however, a fact that people who constitute the anti-social
> element among the Hindus as also some other communities
> other than Sikh had participated in the riots.[21]

In this sense, the RMC holds that this was not a Hindu-Sikh
riot. This description of the criminal lust for plundering property or

---

[19] Hon. Justice Ranganath, *Report of the Ranganath Misra Commission of Inquiry*,
(August 1986), 31.
[20] Ranganath, *Inquiry*, 9.
[21] Ranganath, *Inquiry*, 17.

murder of the Sikhs is based on the idea that the anti-social working class man capitalises on the conditions of violence and illegality that flourish in Delhi at that time. And, at the same time conflates forms of neighbourliness and sociality within the neighbourhoods with the characterisation of communal violence itself.

This duly constituted anti-social subject then stands for organised violence on the basis of a certain rationality that is not bound by nationalistic affective social ties that compelled every *good* citizen and *ordinary* party member to mourn the assassination of the leader of the nation. Rather the anti-social descends into animalistic desires and hence, contrasted with the genuine mourner. I cite:

> Anti-social gangsters obviously had no mourning to observe. The troubled atmosphere provided them with opportunity to plunder and otherwise satisfy their animal desires and, therefore, the conduct exhibited of the people were the anti-social ruffians and usually not the people of Smt Gandhi's camp or party who were ordinarily likely to exhibit mournful conduct.[22]

Thereby crowds invested with passion are more likely to be seen as "communal," rather than crowds directed with rationality that congeal in the figure of the working class male.

In either case, the targeting of Sikhs by crowds whether governed by passion or rationality, does not position the petitioning Sikhs as innocent victims of unjust violence; rather the RMC acquits itself by staging the gory aspects of the violence against the Sikh community as a "mistake." I quote:

> The identification of the Sikhs with every member of that community living in India and to treat every person of that community at par with the assassins has been an unpardonable and unfortunate mistake.[23]

The construction of the 1984 riots as an unpardonable "mistake" accompanies accounts of the widows of 1984 expressing their sorrow at the assassination of Indira Gandhi.

---

[22] Ranganath, *Inquiry*, 29.
[23] Ranganath, *Inquiry*, 67.

Every Sikh who has appeared before the Commission has expressed extreme sorrow on the assassination of Smt. Gandhi. In the condolence meetings that followed her death many of the Sikhs publicly participated. In a number of affidavits of Sikh victims before the Commission there is specific mention of the fact that assault on her and her consequential death brought generation of widespread sense of gloom and sorrow. Some of the widows who appeared before the commission did narrate at length that they were grief stricken when they heard about the assault of Smt Gandhi and her death.[24]

The congealing of the perpetrators into the figure of the "anti-social," the erasure of the evidence of organised violence and the reduction of the events to a "mistake" converted the testimony to the 1984 violence to a public display of allegiance to a slain leader. In a truly Kafkaesque way, the testimony is converted into an "apology" for "provoking" the violence that the witness testified to, and the survivors constituted as a body population that were mistakenly assumed to be provocateurs.[25]

The Nameless Mob

While the appellate discourse on the "crowd" refers to criminological theories of diminished responsibility resulting in the figure of a "demented" rioter in throes of "communal delirium," the anonymous, unidentifiable mob is *produced* at another site of the law. This has pernicious effects on the outcomes of riot cases. Grover's[26] comparison of the legal response to the 1984 violence in Delhi and the violence in Gujarat 2002 is exceedingly important to understand how the "mob" is produced through the *suspension* of

---

[24] Ranganath, *Inquiry*, 68.

[25] This may be contrasted with the *mafipatrak* (letter of apology) that Muslims have been made to sign in Gujarat [see Vrinda Grover, "The Elusive Quest for Justice: Delhi 1984 to Gujarat 2002" in *Gujarat: The Making of a Tragedy*, Siddharth Vardharajan (ed.) [New Delhi: Penguin, 2002 (b)], 358]. Likewise, the circulation of the word "compro," an abbreviation for compromise, has been noted by the IIJ team, which implied that Muslim men and women were made to compromise to withdraw complaints from courts of law in order to return to their neighbourhoods [see International Initiative for Justice Report, *Threatened Existence: A Feminist Analysis of the Genocide in Gujarat* (Bombay: New Age Printing Press, 2003)].

[26] Vrinda Grover, *Quest for Justice: 1984 Massacre of Sikh Citizens in Delhi* [Unpublished Report, 2002 (a)].

ordinary investigative procedures of policing prescribed in the Criminal Procedure Code (CrPC). The first instance of testifying to what happened must be initiated at a local police station which has jurisdiction over the area where the crime was committed, usually entailing the residential localities where the violence took place. In order to report the violence in Gujarat 2002, the survivors had to complain 'to the same police force which had at best been indifferent bystanders and at worst actively colluded in, connived at and instigated the killing and looting of the Muslim community.'[27] We know that initially very few survivors lodged First Information Reports (FIRs). The survivors, in hiding or in refugee camps, would have had to risk their lives to report the crimes. Grover says that 'the police seized this opportunity to record FIRs without consulting the victims. Most of these record general facts and accuse no one in particular.'[28] The nameless mob was produced by the Gujarat police through other techniques such as refusing to register the FIRs, refusing to carry out Test Identification Parades[29] or omitting the names of the perpetrators.

We know from the Delhi 1984 trials that the effects of producing a nameless mob are pernicious[30] since 'in many cases relating to the 1984 massacres, the accused were acquitted due to the non-mentioning of the accused in the FIR.'[31] The most 'innovative' method of producing nameless mobs has been the 'recording of omnibus/running FIRs.'[32] I cite Grover's analysis of Gujarat 2002:

> As in Delhi, 1984, the police adopted an innovative and illegal method of registering FIRs. Instead of registering a separate and distinct FIR with regard to each and every cognizable offence, single omnibus FIR is recorded. The con-

[27] Grover, "The Elusive Quest...," 358.

[28] Grover, *Quest for Justice*, 258.

[29] In the absence of the Test Identification Parade [TIP], no evidentiary value accrues to a witness identifying an accused for the first time in court. Grover (2002b) cites the instance of Harbhajan Kaur who could have identified the perpetrators, if the police had carried out the TIP in 1984. After eleven years, she could not identify the perpetrators in court. In the 1984 trials, the lack of TIP led to the dismissal of cases since the benefit of the doubt went to the accused.

[30] Moreover, the police often *weaken* cases by changing the offence to a lesser one.

[31] Grover, "The Elusive Quest...," 362-3.

[32] Grover , ibid., 363.

tents are general, vague and bereft of details. The incidents reported therein relate to different places, time and accused persons. Some FIRs have been registered where the accused are both Hindus and Muslims and have been booked as part of the same mob. In one FIR, totally unconnected events are clubbed together. The events are spread over several places and at times over several days. ... in November 1984 a similar omnibus FIR was recorded for the colony of Trilokpuri in Delhi where over 200 Sikhs had been slaughtered and burnt within forty eight hours. The investigating officers, while deposing before the trial court, admitted, "that there were oral instructions of his senior officers that all incidents of riots are to be clubbed together and to be dealt under FIR No. 426 and no separate case was being registered."[33]

In the 1984 case *State v Kishori,* the trial court had to 'instruct the police to split the FIR and file separate challans (records) for separate incidents and places.'[34] The production of the "omnibus" FIR is premised on the anticipation of the trial and weakening of evidence. At this site, the law produces an anonymous marauding crowd and the failure of law to deal with communal violence is then accorded to the *nature* of violence itself. The suspension of the law is made manifest as traces of police culpability enter judgments as spectral presences of sanctioned illegal violence during the dark times of riots.[35] This is instanced in the 1984 trial judgment when the ASJ SN Dhingra in *State v Ved Prakash etc* cites the statement of the accused as follows:

> In his statement under section (u/s) 313 CrPC accused Kishori had stated that police made pronouncements in the area that those who had looted the houses of Sikhs, they should put looted articles on the road. These statements were made by Inspector Rathi who was from the Special staff. These announcements were made after police had come to block number 32.... Thus, from this statement of accused u/s

---

[33] Grover, ibid., 363.

[34] Grover, ibid., 365.

[35] The fact that the police followed illegal methods to recover property that had been looted or the fact that the police had illegally confiscated weapons or arms that the Sikhs could have used as weapons of self defence has also been noted by Justice Ranganath Misra.

313 CrPC it is clear that police was in league with accused persons and riot was a consequence of this league.[36]

We see how the illegality of custodial violence enters the writing of judgments. Yet, this "illegibility" of the state[37] such as the actions and words of police officers during the 1984 riots remains spectral in judicial discourse.[38]

Engendering the Riot

The representation of the violent mob in appellate judgments represses the gendered nature of communal violence in many different ways. While there are appellate judgments that note that hate speech against specific communities include fictive accounts of women of a particular community being raped by the other community as a ploy to incite communal violence, we are faced by a peculiar judicial silence on the actual instances of rape of women during such episodes of communal riots. None of the appellate judgments that I collated involving prosecutions against men accused of rioting adjudicated the prosecution of rape in the context of communal violence in the last 18 years. In other words, there has been a systemic failure

---

[36] Cited in Grover, "The Elusive Quest...," 372.

[37] Veena Das and Deborah Poole, (eds.), *Anthropology in the Margins of the State*, (Santa Fe: School of American Research Press, 2004).

[38] The sanctioning of illegal state violence has found critique in another domain of law. Constitutional tort law, which has seen recent judicial innovations especially in cases dealing with riots, holds the state vicariously liable for failing to prevent violence against ordinary citizens. In *M/S Inderpuri General Store & Others v Union of India and Another* it was held that the 'maintenance of law and order is the duty of a responsible government who could not abdicate this function and allow the life and liberty of the citizens in jeopardy' [*AIR 1992 Jammu and Kashmir 11 at 14*]. The Supreme Court has also held that the 'right to protection against any sort of violence or mob frenzy or communal frenzy and breach of any such right is breach of fundamental right for which state is answerable to all individuals more particularly to the living injured or victims of such violence. ... The state within the meaning of article 21 ...cannot be permitted to contend that it is helpless or beyond control to provide protection to all individuals ... In my opinion, there does exist an obligation to provide protection to all persons against any violence or apprehension of violence' [cited in Usha Ramanathan, "Tort Law," *Annual Survey of Indian Law*, Vol. XXXIII-IV, (1997-1998), 607]. The illegibility of the law, then, is brought under the realm of public law through the doctrine of vicarious liability of the state by bracketing the sanctioned illegal violence of the state in order to carry out the function of restoring legitimacy to the state. The fixing of liability then becomes a way by which state law presents itself as a guarantor of constitutional rights.

to record the testimony to rape by women who survive riots. Nor has appellate jurisprudence met the challenges of prosecuting rape during riots.[39]

In the case of prosecutions of everyday forms of rape, women's sexual and reproductive histories have been translated into narrow readings of chastity and loyalty to male notions of sexual morality. The absence of prosecutions of rape in the context of communal violence suggests that the rape law systemically deters women's sexual and reproductive histories to record historical wrongs inscribed on their bodies in the name of the nation. It seems as if women's sexual biographies are continually folded back and read within the discourses of kinship and alliance, and when these are not legible within the discourses of kinship and alliance, there is a deafening judicial silence on what happens to women when they are raped during communal violence.[40] The gap between representations of rape in hate publications and actual instances of rape produces an iconography of difference, which situates raped survivors outside notions of citizenship and nation.

To illustrate this iconography of difference let us briefly turn to Babu Rao v State (Delhi Administration).[41] In this case, the Court held that the text under adjudication was neither a political thesis nor a historical tract rather it fell under the definition of mischief as per Sec. 153 A and 153 B, IPC. Typically, the "Tale of Two Communalism" held that communalism was an instrument used by a militant Muslim minority. It propagated the view that Muslims as a race are violent and rapacious unlike the Hindus - the latter characterised by the absence of intolerance and thirst for blood. The Court held

---

[39] Lawyers, as we know from accounts gathered during the violence in Gujarat 2002, do not consider rape, as grave an offence as murder. Lawyers also claim that prosecutions of rape are much more difficult than murder. Moreover, the police in Gujarat did not register most complaints of rape nor were women sent for medico-legal examinations. After the violence, the condition of women in camps was appalling. Women were not treated for trauma or vaginal infections, STD, HIV/AIDs, abortions or pregnancies in the camps. The rhetoric of denial accompanied testimony after testimony of the most chilling accounts of sexual violence, as the mass rape was denied as a lie in the parliament. Few cases of rape were registered and are currently under trial.

[40] See Veena Das, "Sexual Violence, Discursive Formations and the State," *Economic and Political Weekly*, XXXI (35, 36 and 37), (1996): 2411-23.

[41] AIR 1980 SC 763.

that this text was designed to create hatred and ill-will on the grounds of community.[42] The picture of the perpetrator as a bloodthirsty assailant blinded by communal frenzy is further complicated when we encounter the populist discourses of Hindutva ideologues, which position the Muslim male as racially rapacious. Many historians have noted that the "other" or the community or group in opposition is often symbolised as a rapist. 'Thus in radical race discourse the rapist was a European, in Hindu nationalist and communal discourses he was a Muslim.'[43] In the case of the typical communal riot between Hindus and Muslims, such positioning of the aggressive and rapacious Muslim male subject may be read alongside the elisions in appellate judgments of the rapacious character of the violent crowd during communal violence.

While ordinary rape prosecutions often refer to men's animal desires, and natural sexual instinct that overpowers them temporarily after having met a provocateur in the woman raped, if we look at the construction of the crowd in the judgments on the 1984 violence we find a curious and sustained lack of engagement with such constructions of natural male sexual instinct. For instance, the absence of rape in legal records of communal violence during the 1984 violence suggests that the crowds were seen primarily as male mobs that attacked Sikh men. The animal nature of men actualising in an uncontrollable sexual instinct – the latter the subject of rape in law – is not a matter of adjudication here. In fact, we may even argue that the legal discourse feminises the crowd as a site of temporary, animalistic passion, and thereby divests the crowd of the politics of masculinity that underlies the systemic and structural use of techniques of violence.

---

[42] This precedent is overturned in the well-known "Samana" case. The Bombay High Court held that the Samana editorial that appeared in the Marathi newspaper in the aftermath of the demolition of the Babri Masjid did not promote ill-will and hatred amongst communities, since it did not address Muslims in general but only those anti-national Muslims who did not join the mainstream (read: Hindutva) notions of progress and development (see *Joseph Bain D'Souza and another v State of Maharashtra* 1995 Cri L J 1316).

[43] Samita Sen, "Honor and Resistance: Gender, Community, Class in Bengal 1920-40" in *Bengal: Communities, Development and States*, S. Bandhopadhyay, A. Das Gupta and W. Schendel (eds.) (Delhi: Manohar Publishers, 1994), 209.

Hence, when we read the appellate judgments concerning communal riots we find that judgments are sanitised of the pornography of the riot, whereby sexualised hate speech, which accompanies the description of violence positioning the "other" as rapable, is shorn off from descriptions of violence by male mobs. For instance, testimonies to the Srikrishna Commission[44] indicate that the threat of rape was accompanied by repeated verbal abuse, as is evident by the word "landya" (a castrated male) used to characterise Muslim men. Mehta[45] shows how such characterisations of Muslim men as castrated subjects denudes them of their masculinity and how unspeakable sexual violence was inscribed on the bodies of Muslim men during the 1992-3 violence in Bombay.

The sexualised violence that Muslim men endured does not enter the legal discourse as a fariyad (complaint), rather through the practices of policing 'the body of the Muslim male becomes a commodity.'[46] The police position the individual Muslim body as 'an invariant of the bodies of all Muslim males, irrespective of individual pasts and futures. This closure has a double effect: it produces an abstraction of the male Muslim body (as landya) and it decomposes the body into bits and pieces (as underdeveloped penis, impotent, hunch-backed, bearded and so on). These body parts then circulate in a system of equivalence by which one male Muslim body can be substituted by another.'[47] We do not however encounter the body of the wounded and injured body of Muslim male in the descriptions of the "animal" nature of male crowds in appellate judgments, which fall short of describing this system of equivalence produced through practices of policing. Legal discourse then ignores the acts of commission or omission by the police or other state functionaries that produce a rape culture,[48] while denying that rape is a dominant tech-

---

[44] Hon. Justice.Srikrishna, *Report of the Srikrishna Commission Appointed for Inquiry into the Riots at Mumbai During December 1992 and January 1993*, (Vol. I and II, Published privately by Jyoti Punwani and Vrijendra, 1998).

[45] Deepak Mehta, "Communal Violence, Public Spaces and the Unmaking of Men" (First presented at "Travelling Seminar on Exploring Masculinities" organised by Aakar and UNIFEM, Vadodara, 19-20 December, 2001, Revised Paper, 2003).

[46] Mehta, 'Unmaking of Men,' 25.

[47] Ibid.

[48] Baxi argues that 'there is not *much* that constitutional governance can achieve except to *normalize violence*, almost as a social cost of doing democratic politics.

nique of violence deployed by crowds.[49] While we know that the existing laws on sexual violence remain inadequate to redress the suffering of rape on women, children and men during communal violence, even the existing descriptions of communal violence that we encounter in appellate judgments are purged of the contexts of sexual violence.

I argue further that the elision of the effects of the crowd violence negates the suffering of sexual violence during communal violence in order to institute the difference between a riot and genocide. I wish to demonstrate this point by turning to the 1984 violence in Delhi. We find that in the aftermath of the 1984 violence, 'not a single case of molestation or rape was ever registered.'[50] A number of fact-finding reports published in the aftermath of Delhi 1984 reported narratives of rape of women, yet these did not enter legal records.[51] Kishwar[52] states that while very few Sikh women were killed during the violence with the exception of women trapped in burning houses, Sikh women witnessed the murder of the male members of their families. Kishwar records evidence of gang rape of women by the attacking mobs. She states that older women were raped in front of their families. Young female children were not spared either. When

---

This logic articulates what must be named as "rape culture." Rape culture signifies ways of doing competitive party politics and managing governance *in which brutal collective sexual assaults on women remain enclosed in contrived and escalating orders of impunity.* In an operative rape culture, then women's right to *be* and *remain* human depends not on the normative necessity of the law or the constitution but on the contingent necessities of the politics of fraud and force. Rape culture names violence against women as a situation of "misfortunate" not as an act of "*injustice.*" Rape cultures flourish when organized political violence is regarded as a situation of misfortune because *even* good governance may not be said to prevent misfortunes. In contrast, naming organized violence as an act of injustice summons action and struggle; and renders governance illegitimate.' Upendra Baxi, "The Gujarat Catastrophe: Notes on Reading Politics as Democidal Rape Culture," in *The Violence of Normal Times: Essays on Women's Lifeworlds*, Kalpana Kannabiran (ed.) (Women Unlimited: New Delhi 2005), 336.

[49] Also see Upendra Baxi, "The Second Gujarat Catastrophe," *Economic and Political Weekly*, XXXVII (14), (2002): 3519-3531.

[50] Grover, *Quest for Justice*, 111.

[51] See Uma Chakravarti and Nandita Haksar (eds.), *The Delhi Riots: Three days in the life of a Nation* (New Delhi: Lancer International, 1987), Amiya Rao, "When Delhi Burnt," *Economic and Political Weekly* (December 8, 1984): 2066-69, Kishwar, 'Gangster Rule.'

[52] Madhu Kishwar interviewed women from Trans Yamuna colonies, especially Trilokpuri, in 1984.

Kishwar spoke to GK from Trilokpuri, she learnt that 7-8 men had raped GK, who was 45 years old in 1984. GK testified to the fact that almost every woman and female child was raped in her neighbourhood during the 1984 violence. The stigma that accrues to admitting to rape prevented women, especially unmarried young women, from testifying to mass rape. I quote:

> ... those women in whose homes there is one or more surviving man cannot make a public statement because that will be dishonouring those men. I have no one left. My daughter has also been widowed. My daughter-in-law who has three children has also been widowed. Another daughter-in-law was married only one and a half months ago and has also been widowed. I have nothing left. That is why I want to give my statement.[53]

The testimony to rape during the violence is inflected through discourses of shame and honour, such that making rape public would mean dishonouring and bringing shame to the only surviving men in the extended family.

The testimony of IB who was forcibly incarcerated with other women after the men had been killed and their houses had been burnt down is chilling. I quote:

> We women all huddled together and they offered us some water. As we were drinking water, they began dragging off whichever girl they liked. Each girl was taken away by a gang of 10 or 12 boys, many of them in their teens. They would take her to a nearby masjid, gang rape her and send her back after a few hours. Some never returned. Those who returned were in a pitiable condition and without a stitch of clothing. One young girl said 15 men had climbed on her.[54]

This account details the temporary formation that approximates what have been called "rape camps," where women are forcibly incarcerated with the intent to rape them in order to destroy the community.

---

[53] Kishwar, 'Gangster Rule,' 14.
[54] Ibid., 15.

While some women did not report rape due to the fear of bringing shame and dishonour to their surviving families, others did come forward with complaints. Kishwar tells us that women did complain of rape to doctors in the camps that were set up, for instance, in Farsh Bazaar.[55] According to one rape survivor,

> Most of the women who went to register a case were young, unmarried women. Four of them were sent into the doctor's room. I was asked to wait outside. The women who went inside were intimidated by those in charge and were warned not to undergo the medical examination. They were told that hands would be shoved up their vaginas and much else would be done to them. They being young, inexperienced women got frightened and did not insist on a medical examination.[56]

This account speaks of how the basic premise of criminal law that rape, as a cognizable offence, is a serious offence and prompt medical attention must be provided to the survivor, is violated. Whereas the medical convention of the "two-finger" test[57] which entails the insertion of two fingers in the vagina, with the consent of the woman, to record whether the hymen is distensible or not was used to intimidate rape survivors. The deployment of the two finger test as a threat of further sexual violence within the confines of a

---

[55] The Farsh Bazaar camp was an emergency response to the 1984 violence in Delhi. According to Darryl D'Monte, 'as many as 2,000 people had sought safety in the Farsh Bazaar police station; the Station House Officer there was most helpful – in sharp contrast to the majority of the police who either looked the other way or actually connived at the arson and murder. ...The SHO turned a newly built and unoccupied police colony nearby into an instant relief camp, very probably, it was on November 3 evening, the very first in Delhi' ["How Concerned Citizens Tackled Delhi Riots," *Economic Political Weekly*, (November 17, 1984), 1944].

[56] Kishwar, 'Gangster Rule,' 16.

[57] The two-finger test, a medical convention that survives colonial medical jurisprudence is used routinely to ascertain whether the hymen has been destroyed or not. It is then translated to suggest whether a woman is habituated to sex or not. This then finds translation in courts to ascertain a woman's sexual history, depending on whether she is unmarried or married. Sexual history then has been used as evidence for discrediting the testimony of rape. In case a woman refuses the two-finger test, her testimony may be considered suspect. However, this does not mean that medical examination is confined to the two-finger test or the doctors can use the two-finger test to intimidate women into withdrawing their complaints. Nor can doctors withdraw medical treatment on these grounds.

doctor's room in a camp translates a clinical practice into a technique of sexual violence. We may note here the relationship between the uses of clinical practice of two-finger test as a technique by which rape is routinely converted into consensual sex in ordinary criminal trials with complaints of rape in camps in the aftermath of communal violence as an effective way of threatening traumatised women with further sexual violence. We must bear in mind then that the threat of sexual violence against women by medico-legal experts among other state functionaries in the aftermath of communal violence is an important cause for the lack of registration of complaints of rape.

The sexualised nature of the violence that women who survived 1984 endured has denuded redressal even while women were positioned as the survivors who testified to the violence against their male family members. The circumscription of the violence against women in 1984 names married women who lost their husbands [and other male family members] as "widows." The married woman survivor is therefore named as a widow of 1984, and widowhood becomes the privileged route through which women enter judicial reckoning as witnesses and survivors. The violence is gendered only to acknowledge that women who lost their men found themselves in situations of economic destitution as primary caregivers of fatherless children in patriarchal social contexts. The emergence of widowhood as a category for compensation, rehabilitation and redressal in legal and administrative discourses that proliferated in the aftermath of the 1984 riots firmly placed women as witnesses to the violence committed against them through the loss of their men. This loss is deployed as a discursive strategy to assume that women were not systemically targeted, and elides the violence they faced. Nor did the courts take into cognisance the fact that lower class Sikh women who testified in courts of law in the aftermath of the 1984 violence were terrorised by threats of rape, and abduction such that they 'were literally assaulted by a continuous violence from every possible direction.'[58]

---

[58] Veena Das, *Mirrors*, 30.

The testimonies of women in trial courts to the murder of members of their family suggest traces of sexual violence that women endured. As Grover says,

> Women were subjected to rape and other brutal sexual assaults but there is till date no official legal record, redressal or acknowledgment of these crimes. A glimpse of the sexual crimes committed against these women can be found in their testimonies before the trial court, when they came to depose in cases pertaining to the murder of their family members. Women have described in their evidence before the court how attackers tried to strip them and they offered valuables to save their honour and then the statement abruptly ends.[59]

Likewise, we find that Bhakti Bai's testimony against Kishori and others indicates how rape, euphemistically alluded to as a threat to dishonour appears in her narration of what happened to her husband. The Supreme Court held that while Bhakti Bai was unable to 'state what happened to her husband when she was asked to leave her husband on the threat of dishonouring her' but she was 'definite that her husband was killed. Her version appears natural and probable when she stated that a mob attacked her house and there was threat to the lives and honour of women, it is quite natural that she had to go out of the house.'[60] This reference to the threat to the lives and honour of women is significant to the way the actions of the violent mob were constructed since it led the Supreme Court to state categorically that the 1984 riots did not amount to genocide.[61] *Kishori v State of Delhi* holds that:

---

[59] Grover, *Elusive Quest*, 376.

[60] *Kishori v State of Delhi* (1999) 1 SCC 148 at 153.

[61] It is pertinent to recall here that the Polish jurist Raphael Lemkin coined the term "genocide," a combination of the Greek word *genos* (race, tribe) with the Latin root *cide* (killing of). The word first appeared in his book entitled *Axis Rule in Occupied Europe*, published in November 1944. He worked tirelessly towards bringing genocide into international law leading the United Nations 'to pass a preliminary resolution (96-I) in 1946 stating that genocide occurs "when racial, religious, political and other groups have been destroyed entirely or in part"' [Alexander Laban Hinton, (ed.), *Annihilating Difference: The Anthropology of Genocide*, (California: California University Press, 2002), 3]. At this time, the category of "political and other groups" was deeply contested and finally was dropped from 'the final version of the 1948 Genocide Convention on the Prevention and Punishment of Genocide, which dealt only with "national, ethnical, racial or religious groups"' (Hinton, *Annihilating*

We may notice that the acts attributed to the mob of which the appellant was a member at the relevant time cannot be stated to be a result of any organized systematic activity leading to genocide. Perhaps, we can visualise that to the extent that the mob wanted to teach a stern lesson to the Sikhs, there was some organisation but in that design, that they did not consider that women and children should be annihilated which is a redeeming feature. When an amorphous group of persons come together, it cannot be said that they indulge in any systematic or organized activity. Such group may indulge in activities and may remain cohesive only after a temporary period and therefore would disintegrate. ...the acts of the mob of which the appellant was a member was only the result of a temporary frenzy.[62]

We are told that killing adult men of a community does not signify systemic destruction of a community in part or in whole. Rather this judgment is inflected by the iconography of genocide as an organised and systematic form of violence that 'annihilates' women and children. Moreover, the violence is constructed as "redeemable" since women and children were not raped and/or killed *systemically*. An implicit and perverse notion of a redeeming *chivalry* runs through these accounts – where women and children are spared on the pain of the threat that if they did not leave their men they would be killed or dishonoured. The underlying notion of *chivalry* is premised on the notion that male violence was directed at punishing unruly Sikh men who had slain a national leader, a woman identified as the mother of the nation, while the threat of rape to Sikh women was assumed to not have met actualisation.

The law did not create the conditions whereby Sikh women could testify to rape. Rather, the *absence* of the testimony to rape in

---

Difference, 3). Genocide has been defined under Article II of the United Nations Genocide Convention, 1948 as follows: 'In the present Convention, genocide means any of the following acts committed with intent to destroy, in whole or in part, a national, ethnical, racial or religious group, as such Killing members of the group; Causing serious bodily or mental harm to members of the group; Deliberately inflicting on the group conditions of life calculated to bring about its physical destruction in whole or in part; Imposing measures intended to prevent births within the group; Forcibly transferring children of the group to another group' (cited in Hinton, *Annihilating Difference*, 3).

[62] (1999)1 SCC at 157.

the records of the courts of appeal was deployed as a discursive strategy to describe the 1984 violence as a riot distinct from genocide. It is for this reason that *Kishori v State of Delhi* becomes significant since the *lack* of 'annihilation of women and children' (read: sexual violence and murder) is used to name the 1984 violence as a riot. In contrast, the discursive shift in the naming of sexual violence during the genocidal violence in Gujarat 2002 has forced open the question of the way the legal discourse on riots silences the experiences of sexual violence, enforced impregnation and the destruction of the foetus of pregnant women.[63]

Adjudicating the Potential of Communal Violence

While the theories of crowd behaviour domesticate the very nature of violence of the communal riot - violence that exceeds the limits of the legal representation of communal riots - the adjudication of public tranquility acts to establish a limit to the power of the unruly mob. It acts as a discursive strategy to restore authority, while moving into the category of governance. The nature of violence that is recognised as typical to a riot accompanies assessments of the restoration of communal harmony. Here, we find that communal harmony is based on judicial interpretation of the state response to the complaints i.e. the number of arrests, the time that has lapsed to demonstrate that people no longer are interested in moving courts for justice and no outbreak of similar scale of violence since the event under adjudication. This legal bureaucratic reckoning of the aftermath of violence is a self-satisfied projection of the state's response to communal violence.

We are told that particular kinds of judgments are imbued with the capacity to disturb public tranquility and communal harmony, restored after violent periods marked by riots. Such judgments that address threats to public order are oriented to two different kinds of concerns. First, judges are concerned that the outcome of a judgment could lead to violence. In other words, the judgment itself is seen as a legal event that could produce the conditions for violence. Second, the present context of violence or harmony inflects the

---

[63] See IIJ Report, *Threatened Existence*.

way the event that took place in the past is read.[64] The outcome of the judgment is oriented to its symbolic function in the present socio-political contexts.[65]

Let us turn to the violence against the Muslims in 1992-3 after the demolition of the Babri Masjid in Bombay and Gujarat. While the Srikrishna Report, discussed in this volume by Mehta,[66] has been part of public discourse, it is lesser known that the enquiry committee set up to hear testimonies of violence in Gujarat was wound up. It is to the Gujarat enquiry into the anti-Muslim riots during 1992 that we turn now.

In *Jan Sangharsh Manch v State of Gujarat*,[67] we learn that the public interest litigation (PIL) failed since the court refused to interfere with the government's decision to wind up the committee to investigate the 1992 riots in Gujarat. The facts of the case detailed in the judgment are as follows:

The Government of Gujarat appointed an enquiry commission on 21st December 1992 to 'inquire into the facts and circumstances of the violent incidents and communal riots that took place during 6th to 9th December, 1992 following the demolition of the Babri Masjid. While the Commission was on the verge of completing its final report, the Government refused to grant a further extension

---

[64] The different temporalities that constitute legal time is true for all of judicial interpretation as Fitzpatrick argues, 'the constitution of law is not just its accommodating these different temporalities, it must also match time in their combination. ... In sentencing, for example, the judge is supposed to stand, objectively apart from an inconsistent popular sentiment, especially of the more atavistic kind, yet have a responsive regard to changes in such a sentiment. ... Generally, judges are observed more and more to be giving effect to changing times when making their decisions, yet they never only do that. Rather, they seek to base the decision in the already given' [Peter Fitzpatrick, *Modernism and the Grounds of Law*, (Cambridge: Cambridge University Press, 2001) 89].

[65] For instance, the Justice C.D. Parekh Commission of Inquiry, which had investigated the 1982 Meerut riots, and submitted its report to the Government in 1988, was not acted upon for a decade. A public interest litigation was filed on this issue. The Court directed the Government to take a decision towards implementing the report. The Government rejected the findings of the report in order to 'maintain religious and political harmony in Meerut city and to avert any flare up in any particular class or community' [*Falzalur Rehman v State of U.P.* (1999) 7 SCC 683 at 684].

[66] Deepak Mehta, *Documents and Testimony: Violence, Witnessing and Subjectivity in the Bombay Riots – 1992-93* (2005, in this issue).

[67] AIR 1998 Guj 133.

from 1st July 1997.'[68] The Commission ceased on 30th June 1997. Justice IC Bhatt had been appointed as the Commission on 21st December 1992. He retired when he was appointed as Lokayukta. Subsequently, Justice BM Chauhan, also a retired Judge from the Gujarat High Court, was appointed on 9th December 2003. The petitioners claimed that the government did not appoint the required staff for the Commission, even a stenographer was not provided until middle of 1996. Despite this, the Commission examined nearly 1300 witnesses and accepted 2000 documents. The Commission, which had been granted nine extensions, following the initial six-month period, applied for a four-month extension in order to complete its report. The work of the Commission came to a 'grinding halt' on 30th June 1997.[69] Challenging these claims, the Government of Gujarat argued that the 'it took the decision' to 'wind up the commission' on the following grounds:

> The victims of the violence have been compensated.
> People who have suffered have lodged complaints which were taken care of legally.
> People who have suffered have lodged complaints and procedures under the Criminal Procedure Code have already been initiated.
> Accused found in such cases have been arrested.
> Because of lapse of time people have lost interest.
> No advocates were attending the Commission for cross-examining the officers of the Police Department, who have filed their affidavits.
> There has been communal peace and harmony in the state since the riot of 1992.[70]

The Supreme Court clarified that the Commissions of Inquiry Act, 1952 confers the discretion on governments to appoint enquiry commissions to inquire into matters of public importance. It is settled law that governments cannot be forced to appoint enquiry commissions. Moreover, the court held that:

---

[68] AIR 1998 Guj 133 at 134.
[69] AIR 1998 Guj 133 at 134.
[70] AIR 1998 Guj 133 at 135.

In such a situation the government thought it proper not to have a post-mortem examination of the circumstances which led to the riots for kindling feelings of bickering between members of different communities. This reason appears to be quite justifiable. It cannot be said that it is an irrelevant consideration.[71]

The petitioner's argument that the public must have the right to information regarding the circumstances which led to the riots in 1992, emanating from Article 19 (1) (a) in the Constitution of India (COI), was found to be valid as long as this right was subjected to limitations. These limitations are laid out as follow:

Certain unhappy situations arose in December 1992 following the demolition of the Babri Masjid. Riots took place. People belonging to different communities fought each other. It was more than seven years back. People have forgotten those instances. Peace has been restored. Time being the best healer, by influx (sic) of time people have forgotten those black days. Now at this instance of time if circumstances which led to the riots are brought to light, according to the Government, it will affect communal harmony and peace. These considerations under no circumstance can be termed irrelevant.[72]

The Court did not find any grounds to direct the Gujarat Government to extend the term of the Commission. The Government's stance that legal redressal, and compensation had been provided is a standard motif that occurs in the 1984 judgments as well. Moreover, the idea that survivors of violence loose interest or "forget those instances" pictures the aftermath of the riot as a return to health, after being inflicted by a temporary pathology, by the work of time, as argued by Mehta in this volume. Time is accrued healing properties that allow a resurgence of social commerce between people of different communities. The law is then not seen as a site of commemoration, rather the law must allow the "disinterested" legal subject to forget the past. Remembrance is pictured as a route to revive the 'bickering between communities,' a danger to communal

---

[71] AIR 1998 Guj 133 at 136.
[72] AIR 1998 Guj 133 at 137.

harmony and peace. To allow the public the knowledge of the circumstances of the 1992-3 riots is seen as being tantamount to a post-mortem, an event that must be treated as a cadaver that is not exhumed for forensic analysis, so that the potential of violence in the future could be adjudicated. The description of the violence in 1992-3 as an unhappy situation, whereby public access to the testimonies to violence was marked with a closure must be read alongside the independent enquiries that investigated the testimonies to sexual violence in Surat.[73] This was the period when women's groups for the first time archived extensively the testimonies of sexual violence during communal violence. This archive was oriented to a different notion of future based on evidence of the systemic socialisation of hatred – a future that judicial discourse discounted.

Let us turn to the violence subsequently witnessed in Gujarat 2002, which folds into an Allahabad High Court judgment published in 2003, illustrating how law not merely adjudicates communal harmony but how crimes committed in the past are inflected by the judicial interpretation of the present in order to adjudicate communal harmony. I consider the instance when one Shaukat Ali challenged the order of detention (dated 3-1-2002) under the National Security Act (65 of 1980) S. 3 in the Allahabad High Court. He was detained on the grounds that he 'slaughtered a cow and the knife and rods were recovered from him. This incident caused communal tension and hence the impugned detention order was passed.'[74] The judgment is terse in stating that there was no delay in deciding the petitioner's representation and the detention order was upheld on the following grounds:

> Communal amity and harmony are absolutely essential for the progress of the nation. We cannot afford to have another Gujarat in U.P. Slaughter of cows hurts the sentiments of the Hindus and hence should not be committed. In our opinion cow slaughter affects public order because it is likely to incite communal tension. Hence, it is not merely the case of law and order.[75]

---

[73] See Tanika Sarkar and Urvashi Butalia (eds.), *Women and the Hindu Right: A Collection of Essays* (New Delhi: Kali for Women, 1995).
[74] *Shakaut Ali v Union of India* 2003 Cri LJ 235.
[75] 2003 Cri LJ at 235-236.

This adjudication of communal amity and harmony reads the potential of *another Gujarat* by reading *provocation* in acts that hurt Hindu sentiments typified by cow slaughter.

We must note here that the distinction between law and order as versus public order is clearly spelt in cases dealing with preventive detention cases. The Gujarat High Court (GHC) cites *Arun Ghosh v West Bengal*[76] in *Vijay Rambrij Yadav v Ahmedabad City and Ors*[77] albeit here the petition of the detenu fails. The GHC distinguishes between public order and law and order by citing the following illustration found in *Arun Ghosh v West Bengal*:

> Take the case of assault on girls. A guest at a hotel may kiss or make advances to half a dozen chambermaids. He may annoy them and also the management but he does not cause disturbance of public order. He may even have a fracas with one of the friends of the girls but even then it would be a case of breach of law and order only. Take another case of a man who molests (*sic*) a woman in lonely places. As a result of his activities girls going to colleges and schools are in constant danger. Women going for their ordinary business are afraid of being waylaid and assaulted. The activity of this man in its essential quality is not different from the act of the other man but in its potentiality and its effect on public tranquility there is a vast difference. The act of the man who molests girls in lonely places causes disturbances in the even tempo of public order. His act makes all women apprehensive of their honour and he can be said to be causing disturbance of public order and not merely committing individual actions which may be taken note of by criminal prosecution agencies.[78]

While this judgment is pronounced before the recent appellate innovations suggesting guidelines to redress sexual harassment of women at the workplace,[79] it clarifies that the distinction does not lie in the *nature* of violence but in its potential *effects* on society as a

---

[76] [1970] 1 SCC 98.
[77] 1993(1) GLH 477.
[78] *Vijay Rambrij Yadav v Ahmedabad City and Ors* 1993(1) GLH 477 at 482.
[79] *Vishakha and Anrs v. Union of India* AIR 1997 SC 3011.

whole as versus those on an individual.[80] Cow slaughter may then amount to a law and order problem, however when it is read as a threat to public order we learn that a person may be jailed without trial under the preventive detention laws. Thus, we see that the juridical assessments of the potential rather than the "quality" of the event to prevent violence mark the power of state law.[81]

The use of preventive detention laws to adjudicate the potential of communal violence is part of the systemic processes of using the law to produce conditions of communal violence. When we look at the Prevention of Anti Social Activities Act (PASA), a local law applicable in Gujarat, we find that the appellate courts have developed several standards for preventing the indiscriminate incarceration of legal subjects without a trial by local state functionaries.[82] These judgments illustrate offences ranging from bootlegging to inciting communal tension.[83] The Gujarat High Court criticised the practice of releasing a PASA detenu on parole during specific times such as certain religious festivals, where the detenu would violate the very condition for which he was detained.[84] Consider the case moved by a

---

[80] The GHC has also relied on *Arun Ghosh v West Bengal* which held that 'public order is the even tempo of the life of the community as a whole or even a specified locality. Disturbance of public order is to be distinguished from acts directed against individuals who do not disturb the society to the extent of causing a general disturbance and its effect upon the life of the community in a locality which determines whether the disturbance amounts only to a breach of law and order. An Act by itself is not determinant of its own gravity. In its quality it may not differ from another but in its potentiality it may be so very different' [cited in *State of Gujarat v Dawood Jiwan Solanki* 1997 (2) GLH Vol XVII (2) 57 at 66].

[81] For instance, in another judgment from Gujarat High Court, which cites an earlier ruling, we learn that 'when communal tension is high, an indiscreet act of no significance is likely to disturb or dislocate the even tempo of the life of the community. An order of detention made in such a situation has to take note of the potentiality of the act objected to' [*Mohmad Salim @ Salim Khan Ikbalhusen Pathan v Police Commissioner* 1997(1) GLH Vol XVII (1) 341 at 345].

[82] The GHC held that, 'in such matters when life and liberty of the citizens are put in jeopardy without trial and detention orders are passed, the approach at no stage should be casual. Higher the power greater should be the restraint and caution particularly in the matters on detention' [*Mohamad Sarif @ Kalio, Nurmohmadsarnibapu Shaikh v Commissioner of Police*, Ahmedabad & Ors 1997 (1) GLH 1017].

[83] The PASA judgments reveal that the figure of the detenu moves between two poles: the victimised legal subject who may occupy various subject positions such as woman, tribal, Muslim, lower caste, refugee and so on, or detenu as the hardened criminal or the policeman - who is knowingly let out on parole.

[84] See *Dilip Kumar Amritlal v DM Rajkot*, 1992 (2) GLR 1471.

PASA detenu, who argued that his rights under Article 226, COI had been violated.[85] In this case, we learn that the detenu, a suspended police employee who 'created an atmosphere of terror and horror in the city of Baroda,' challenged the legality and validity of the order of detention, dated Aug 24, 1992 passed by the Commissioner of Police under sec 3 (2) of PASA. The Court remarked that the invocation of the power to detain the accused was essential and not faulted. However, the Government allowed temporary release to the detenu,

> ... without any justifiable cause so that when the innocent persons are in a mood to celebrate the religious festival, a reign of terror and atmosphere of havoc and panic is created by this detenu by causing grievous and fatal injuries to the persons and irreparable harm of their properties.[86]

The Court further held that 'the government has been so callous and indifferent to its positive duty to the innocent citizens and has been so active in extending its protective umbrella to hardened criminals that it has shown little respect to the judgment of this court.'[87] The court released the detenu on the grounds that 'if the purpose of preventive detention is to detain the detenu from carrying on or indulging in nefarious deadly criminal activities, his temporary release for no justifiable cause would establish that there was no reason to detain him.'[88] This suggests that preventive detention functions as the mode by which legitimacy is restored by making arrests of specific persons, and defeats the purpose of detention by releasing the detenu on parole at specific periods identified as "sensitive."

This contestation around the adjudication of public tranquility and communal harmony is further complicated when we consider the state response to crowd violence during the communal violence in Ahmedabad in 1985. I recall the chilling events as described in *Dilavar Hussain Mohammadbhai Laliwala v State of Gujarat.*[89] In February 1985, Ahmedabad witnessed the agitation against reservations for the backward castes. This led to communal riots between Hindus

---

[85] See *Sanjaben Shobhrajsinh Siddha v State of Guj & Ors* 1993 (2) GLH 1648.
[86] *Sanjaben Shobhrajsinh Siddha v State of Guj & Ors* 1993 (2) GLH 1648 at 1650.
[87] 1993 (2) GLH 1648 at 1651.
[88] 1993 (2) GLH 1648 at 1652.
[89] 1991 (1) GLH 198 (SC).

and Muslims in Ahmedabad in March 1985. The army was called in April 1985. The criminal appeal we are concerned with here outlined the chain of events that unfolded in Dhabgarwad, a large locality in Ahmedabad, which witnessed a 'riot of shocking magnitude' in March 1985, resulting in mass exodus of Dabgars – a Hindu community which earned its livelihood by manufacturing musical instruments and also umbrellas and kites. After the army was stationed and 'calm partially restored' some Dabgars came back, while others used to come during the day to look after their property and business. Maniben, a dagbar, continued to live in the neighbourhood since she had nowhere to go and believed that she would not come to any harm. One of her daughters had married a Muslim man, although at that time her daughter had strained relations with her husband. On 9th June 1985, the military left. On the same day,

> Members of the minority community ... intermingled in the corner somewhere near the house of Maniben... they indulged in most cowardly and shameful act or pushing open the door of the house setting fire to it and then chaining it from outside resulting in the death of the lady, her two daughters, four grandchildren and son of a neighbour. Next house set ablaze was of Navin and then many others.[90]

The Court commenting on the event said:

> Neighbours residing peacefully for generations sharing common happiness and sorrow even playing cricket together suddenly went mad. Blood thirsty for each other. Burning, looting and killing became the order of the day. Even ladies attempted to prevent fire brigade from extinguishing fire. How pathetic and sad.[91]

The Supreme Court further held that 'even sadder was the manner in which the machinery of law moved.'[92] The accused were chargesheeted for constituting an unlawful assembly comprising of 1500-2000 people. The number of people accused for forming the

---

[90] 1991 (1) GLH 198 (SC) at 201.
[91] 1991 (1) GLH 198 (SC) at 199.
[92] 1991 (1) GLH 198 (SC) at 199.

unlawful assembly came down to 150-200 during evidence. The charge was framed against 63 under TADA[93] and various offences including s. 302 IPC. Out of 63 accused, 56 were acquitted due to lack of evidence or insufficient evidence. The Court remarked, 'what an affront to fundamental rights and human dignity. Liberty and freedom of these persons was in chains for more than a year. For no reason. One even died in confinement.'[94]

This appeal was de-linked from the adjudication waiting before the Constitution Bench assailing the trial under TADA Act,

> Because of the ACT being *ultra vires* of the fundamental right guaranteed under Constitution and absence of circumstances justifying its extension to the State of Gujarat ... Invoking of provisions of TADA Act, in communal riot, was attacked and it was submitted that a combined reading of Secs 3 and 4 with explanation indicated that the legislative intention was to confine the applicability of the Act to secessionist or insurgency activities against the state and not to ordinary crimes for which provisions exist in the penal code.[95]

The Supreme Court found that the prosecution version suffered from serious infirmities and there was no option but to acquit the accused. The Court held that:

> We, however, hope that our order shall bring good sense to members of both the communities residing in Dabgarwad and make them realise the disaster which such senseless riots result in and they shall in future take steps to avoid recur-

---

[93] The promulgation of the Terrorist and Disruptive Activities (Prevention) Act, 1985 (TADA), marked the beginning of extraordinary laws that brought the jurisprudence of the riot in the realm of laws against terrorism. In 1985, TADA came into force as a "temporary" legislation that called for a review after two years, with the view to deal with the "exceptional" circumstances that led to the promulgation of the law. It was reviewed by the legislature after two years. On May 24, May 1987, the Terrorist and Disruptive Activities (Prevention) Act, 1987 was enacted. This law was extended after review until May 23, 1995. The Prevention of Terrorism Act (POTA) replaced this law in 2000.

[94] 1991 (1) GLH 198 (SC) at 199.

[95] 1991 (1) GLH 198 (SC) at 199-200.

rence of such incidents and try to resort to the atmosphere that prevailed before March 1985.[96]

I wish to make two points here. First, the description of bloodthirsty rioters is noteworthy in its reference to "minority" women as rioters, explicitly referring to the fact that women joined to assist the rioting mob or preventing aid to the victims of the mob. This is in contrast to the recent literature that has detailed the rise in the ranks of women in Hindutva organisations, which does not enter the description of communal riots in appellate judgments.[97] Second, blame is approportioned on both the communities making an extraordinary equivalence between crowd violence and the sanctioned illegal violence of the state as a consequence of the crowd violence. The admonition to the Hindus and Muslims residing in Dabgarwad places the blame on the communities for deserting sense. The Hindus, we are told suffered horrendous forms of communal violence at the hands of the 'minority' community and the Muslims - one of whom died awaiting the trial - made victims by the legal process for no reason. The suspension of the law during the 1985 violence in Gujarat, the alliances between criminals, police and politicians or the "misuse" of TADA to discipline an entire community is elided by this pernicious chide. This sanctioned illegal violence of the state – the state's response to crowd violence – makes law illegible to these legal subjects now named as terrorists.

Conclusion

In this paper, I have shown how judicial discourse portrays the "riot" as invested in frenzied collectivities. Judicial discourse naturalizes certain forms of violence, by attributing them to communal riots, while it elides other forms of violence. In this way, such discourse sanction the illegal use of violence by the state - either by acts of commission or omission. Judicial discourse ascribes the inability to prosecute such crimes to the nature of the violence while disregarding the role of the state in producing the nameless mob. Moreover, judicial discourse *feminises* crowd violence thereby successfully

---

[96] 1991 (1) GLH 198 (SC) at 206.
[97] Sarkar and Butalia, *Women and the Hindu Right.*

silencing testimonies to sexual violence during communal violence, and at the same time uses this absence of recorded testimony as a discursive strategy to distinguish riots from genocidal violence. The continued positioning of communal riots as violence produced due to the timeless and primordial hatred between communities without considering the role of the state in executing mass murders, and mass rape, accords the state greater powers to resort to violence. This is in sharp contrast to the attempt on the part of lawyers, activists and scholars to name the violence in Gujarat 2002 as an infringement of cosmopolitan laws[98] on genocide and as crimes against humanity.

I have argued that the judicial discourse on violent crowds must be read alongside the way communal harmony is adjudicated. This is important, for judicial assessments of peace or harmony determine how law becomes a site of commemoration. This becomes a point of adjudication when courts legislate how people *remember* a riot in the aftermath of violence when "peace" has been restored. The judicial archive is then oriented to a notion of a future that derives from thinking of riots as temporal aberrations that heal with the passage of time. Certain forms of remembrance are constituted as a threat to public tranquility and, documents such as enquiry committee reports and even judgments, which are oriented to the future, are seen as being invested with the power of inciting further violence.

The work of ordinary and extraordinary law then creates the sphere of that which is justiciable and that which can only appear in appellate judgments as spectral presences. The deployments of extraordinary laws that have encroached upon ordinary laws have named communal violence as an act of terror, and subsequently aligned themselves with global discourses on terror. With the recent shifts that have named communal violence as an act of terror, we see the expanding possibilities of body populations brought under the subjection of law through extraordinary laws, and how global dis-

---

[98] Cosmopolitan law is distinct from international law, which is the 'system of regulation that governs the relationships between states, while cosmopolitan law is a development of this into a new entity. Cosmopolitan law is the emerging body of law that aims to protect the human rights of individuals and groups, primarily from serious threats that may be posed to them by their 'own' states, by invading states, or other state-like formations… Cosmopolitan law is one response to the inadequacy of nationalism and the actualisation of the nation state' [David Hirsh, *Law against Genocide: Cosmopolitan Trials*, (London: Glasshouse Press, 2003), 12].

courses on terrorism to align with local discourses, which congeal in the figure of the "Muslim." The extraordinary laws of preventive detention adjudicate the potentiality of communal violence while the laws against terrorism bring to bear states of exceptions to certain body populations as a legal response to the supposed legal inability to address communal violence due to its inherent nature. The judicial discourse on communal violence makes equivalences between crowd violence and the state response to crowd violence. The complacent judicial reckoning of the restoration of communal amity and public tranquility is premised on this equivalence.

Pratiksha Baxi *is Assistant Professor at the Centre for the Study of Law and Governance, JNU, New Delhi. Her research interests include legal anthropology, sexual violence and feminism. She has published articles on the juridical discourses on rape and sexual harassment in India.*

Documents and Testimony: Violence, Witnessing & Subjectivity in the Bombay Riots – 1992-93

Deepak Mehta

Abstract
This paper puts together two different elaborations of the communal riot in Bombay – official documents of Hindu-Muslim warfare and the testimony of one survivor of the violence of 1992-93 in Bombay. Surveying the official documents of the riot in the colonial archive and seeing the repetition of its motifs in the official enquiry committee report for the riots of Bombay in 1992-93, the paper argues that official documents describe the riot in the language of epidemics. These documents establish procedures to deal with the onset of the riot, suggest remedies for its causes and establish measures for rehabilitating its victims. The testimony of the survivor of the 1992-93 riots, taken from fieldwork from Dharavi, a slum in Bombay, deals not so much with the acquisition of facts about the violence, as with its integration into the everyday life of the survivor. In putting these two accounts together we find a relationship of exteriority between testimony and official documents. From a second perspective, however, the testimony of the survivor is conditioned by the documentary practices of the colonial and postcolonial state. These practices exercise a formative influence on remembrance.

Whether retrograde or reactive, the term 'communal riot' is thought to be specific to the experiences of violence between Hindus and Muslims in India. But by what procedures does this term describe relations of violence between Hindus and Muslims? What are the means by which the state controls the riot? Does the riot highlight notions of governmentality more than of politics, signaling a shift from people to populations, from culture to demography? This paper is concerned with these issues as a way of addressing a related

Domains 3:102-131 | Copyright © 2007 South Focus Press

question: in the commissions of enquiry reports that follow a riot what explains the absence of collective responsibility in propagating and instigating violence? Taking as my object of analysis the *Report of the Srikrishna Commission* (henceforth SCR) I will focus on its discursive structure, show its resonance with reports generated in colonial India and argue that the SCR is based on an epidemiological theory of violence. This theory excludes individual subjectivities as much as it argues for the anonymous, random and irrational character of violence. What is excluded is the veracity of individual testimony since it is thought that pain and suffering engendered by violence are paralyzed with fear and incomprehension at best, or used as strategic ploys to obtain compensation. I will be considering one such testimony in this paper.

The *Report of the Srikrishna Commission*,[1] authored by Justice Srikrishna, was conducted at the behest of the Maharashtra Government to focus on the causes of the Bombay riots of 1992-93 and later the bomb blasts of March 1993.[2] In the SCR descriptions of violence are frozen. The *Report* locates violence within affected neighborhoods in Bombay and links it to violent mobs fuelled by political parties. The documentary material garnered by the SCR uses a mass of elements (police force, political parties, criminal crowds) that are placed in relation to one another to arrive at a coherent and static account of the violence. The SCR, thus, is a process by which the riot is made monumental.

In contrast to public documents, individual testimonies are based on the act of speaking and demand the subjectivity of the speaking subject. For Agamben testimony is used in at least three senses.[3] The first points to a person who in a trial or lawsuit between

---

[1] Hon. Justice Srikrishna. *Report of the Srikrishna Commission Appointed for Inquiry into the Riots at Mumbai During December 1992 and January 1993*, (Vol. I & II, published privately by Jyoti Punwani and Vrijendra, 1998).

[2] Bombay was renamed Mumbai in 1995. I will refer to the city by its former name. As is well known the riots of 1992-93 followed the destruction of the Babari mosque on 6 December 1992. In the second week of March 1993 a series of bomb blasts ripped through high-profile financial and political establishments in Bombay.

[3] Giorgio Agamben, *Remnants of Auschwitz: The Witness and the Archive* (trans. Daniel Heller-Roazen) (Stanford: Stanford University Press, 1999), 9. By testimony I refer not so much to a written document as to how a particular event of violence is remembered and placed in everyday life. Remembrance itself changes over a period of time. However, I do not wish to set up a distinction between memory and history

two rival parties occupies the position of a third. The second sense designates a person who has lived through something, and can therefore bear witness to it. Finally, testimony presupposes something that pre-exists the person. Its force must be validated and certified. I use testimony in the second and third senses to show that the speaking subject is both witness and survivor. Spoken testimony is premised on the elaboration of a structure of feeling. Its recall allows for the construction of local subjects: the making of a people who think of themselves as belonging to a place. The question is whether individual personal testimonies add up to a collective view. Is the testifier a rhetorical position, based on a chronological narration of recalled experience and speaking always from a first person perspective?[4] I argue that the speech of the testifier is informed by the archive of the communal riot.[5] To the extent that individual testimony is influenced by public documents, we see the force of third person discourses and how through them Hindu-Muslim violence is collectivized as a riot.

Colonial Riots

The history of the communal riot in Bombay can be traced to the end of the 19th century. Hindu-Muslim violence in the Bombay Presidency may be dated to the *East India (Religious Disturbances) Report*, 1894. The discursive structure of this report exercises a formative influence on the writing of Hindu-Muslim riots. In the colo-

---

or to argue that memory critiques conventional historical discourse. My concern is to show the interpenetration of historical narrative and individual remembrance and forgetting.

[4] Ana Douglas, 'Introduction,' in Ana Douglas and Thomas A. Vogler (eds.) *Witness and Memory: The Discourse of Trauma*, (New York and London: Routledge, 2003), 33-34.

[5] The testimony that I will be considering is drawn from fieldwork in a slum in central Bombay called Dharavi. The fieldwork, conducted with a colleague since 1995, has explored the violence of 1992-93 in Bombay, its afterlife and its embedding in the everyday. For further details see Deepak Mehta and Roma Chatterji, 'Boundaries, Names, Alterities: A Case Study of a "Communal Riot" in Dharavi, Bombay,' in *Remaking a World: Violence, Social Suffering and Recovery*, Veena Das, Arthur Kleinman, Margaret Lock, Mamphela Ramphela and Pamela Reynolds (eds.), (Berkeley and Los Angeles: University of California Press 2002); Deepak Mehta, 'Writing the Riot: Between the Ethnography and Historiography of Communal Violence in India,' in *History and the Present,* Partha Chatterjee and Anjan Ghosh (eds.), (New Delhi: Permanent Black 2002); Roma Chatterji, 'Plans, Habitation and Slums-Redevelopment: The Production of Community in Dharavi, Mumbai,' *Contributions to Indian Sociology*, July 2005.

nial archive we find a period of relative quiet from the turn of the century till the 1920s. Beginning in 1928, we find at least one major riot a year till 1944. The colonial archive reports riots in the city of Bombay in 1923, 1928, 1929, 1931, 1932, 1934, 1936, 1937, 1938, 1939, 1940, 1941 and 1944. Together with official enquiry reports, we find a day-by-day unfolding of the riot in the reports of the Commissioner of Police, regular communiqués issued by the Press Department of the Government of Bombay, extensive coverage in the Press, in various Indian languages, including English and in the *Bombay Congress Bulletin*. An impressive list of official reports is produced on Hindu-Muslim violence after 1894. *Instructions for the Guidance of Honorary Magistrates* during disturbances (1929), the elaboration of a riot prevention scheme (1931) and amendments of the Bombay Police Act, 1902 (1938) explicitly formulate Hindu-Muslim violence as an epidemic that must be treated as a problem of law and order. I will read these accounts in conjunction with the SCR.[6]

A Hindu-Muslim riot on 11 August 1893 lasts for three days.[7] The acting police commissioner of Bombay reports that shortly before 1 p.m., after the Friday prayers Muslim worshippers, armed with sticks begin to attack Hindus and the police in the Byculla locality. "Shouts of 'Din, Din' were raised, sticks waved in the air, and a rush was made for the Maruti Temple in the Hanuman Lane."[8] The rioters are driven down Bhendi Bazaar past the Paidhuni Police Chauki. Within the hour riots break out in various other localities and spread with 'astonishing rapidity through almost the whole of the native town. Infuriated mobs of Musalmans surged

---

[6] In reading these reports together with a spoken testimony of a survivor of the Bombay riots of 1992-93 I hope to evade the distinction between memory and history. Walter Ong's [*Orality and Literacy: The Technologizing of the Word* (London: Methuen, 1982)] distinction between oral societies and print culture assumes that presence and origins (oral) are fundamentally separated from history and written language.

[7] After the violence subsides the government orders an enquiry. The report examines communal violence with reference to the anti-cow slaughter movement in Rangoon, Azamgarh and Bombay. Here I will refer to the report as it applies to Bombay.

[8] George Russell, *East India (Religious Disturbances): Copies or Extracts of Reports Relating to the Recent Conflicts between Hindu and Muhammadans in India, and particularly to the Causes which led To them*, (London: Eyre and Spottiswoode 1894), 29.

from street to street, carrying havoc and destruction in all directions.'[9] If the crowds are dispersed from Bhendi Bazaar, they gather at Grant Road and Parel Road. Riots rage through Kamatipura and Clare and Bellasis roads. Falkland Road, Duncan Road and Nal Bazaar are the scene of furious fighting. Troops are requisitioned by late afternoon.

If the first day of the riot belongs to Muslims, the Hindus in the northern parts of Bombay make the second day's attacks. Violence is initiated by mill-hands at Chinchpokli, Arthur and Parel roads, Siwri and Mazgaon. Large mobs of Hindus are dispersed from Grant Road but not before they destroy Muslim houses. By the close of the second day matters improve and by the end of the third day, "the city began to assume its wonted appearance."[10] The zones of the city that are mentioned in the report refer to the 'native' section of Bombay. All subsequent reports delimit Hindu-Muslim violence as falling within these zones. It is almost as if there is a riot geography to such warfare.

The 1894 report provides a chronology of the riot, but also seeks to compare it with the Parsi-Muslim violence of 1874. On both occasions violence is initiated by Muslims in the neighborhood of the Jama Masjid[11] and there is a "direct relation between religious excitement and a resort to violence" but the 'outbreak' of 1874 does not have the same proportions of 1893.[12] In 1874 the 'mob' was easily dispersed, while during the later outbreak the mobs form into organized gangs, especially the Hindu mill-hands of Bombay. This theme of intra-class violence is further developed in the riot inquiry report of 1929.[13] A file of the Home Department of 1936 mentions that in 1929 the immediate cause of the riots is the spread of false rumors of kidnapping of children by Pathans. Hindu mill-hands attack Pathans in the mill area on 2 February. The Pathans retaliate

---

[9] Ibid.

[10] Ibid., 34.

[11] Ibid., 22.

[12] Ibid.

[13] The violence begins on 2 February 1929 and lasts till about 10 March. Violence occurs again on 22 April and continues till 15 May. On 22 April the Government appoints an inquiry committee. *Home Department (Special), Report of the Bombay Riots Inquiry Committee 1929*, in File No. 543 (10) (E) (B) (Maharashtra State Archives, Presidency College, Bombay).

after two days and by the fifth day of February, violence spreads to the city. But the real reason for the attack on the Pathans is that they have taken the place of striking mill-hands at the Sewri oil installations. 'Communist leaders of strikers resented the Pathans' actions, and during January 1929 there were several unprovoked attacks on Pathan workers by the strikers and mill-hands. Presumably, therefore, strike leaders maliciously started the kidnapping rumours.'[14]

But why should violence between factions of the working class be thought of as communal? The answer is tortuous and tenuous. The 1929 *Report* mentions that on 5 February, the violence between Hindu mill-hands and Pathans turned into a communal riot.[15] As a result of the general strike called in April 1928 by the Girni Kamgar Union, later known as the Red Flag Union, inflammatory speeches were made by 'extremist leaders' and these weakened respect for law and order as much as they led to attacks on Pathans. An extract of the speeches is found in Appendix B of the Report. 'The leaders of the Red Flag Union were quite reckless, and their violent speeches found their expression in the differences of the two communities instead of in class hatred.'[16] But nowhere in the Appendix do we find the leaders exhorting workers to attack Muslims.

In the official reports of the 'alms' riot of 1932, colonial records assign a temporal order to the violence. The file of 1936 divides the riot into three phases. In the first violence begins on 14 May and lasts for six days. In the second phase violence begins on 25 May and continues till the 31st. We then find about ten days of stray assaults. Violence resumes on June 10 and gradually lessens. The assault of three Muslims on 26 June marks the beginning of the third phase. Violence subsides on 2 August 1932. "After that date the situation was completely normal."[17] The official Press note of 20

---

[14] *Home Department (Special), Brief Notes on the Communal Riots in Bombay City in 1929 and 1932*, 24 November 1936, in File No. 870 (14) (Maharashtra State Archives, Presidency College, Bombay).

[15] *Home Department (Special), Report of the Bombay Riots Inquiry Committee 1929*, 9, in File no. 543 (10) (E) (B) (Maharashtra State Archives, Presidency College, Bombay).

[16] Ibid., 21.

[17] *Home Department (Special), Brief Notes on the Communal Riots in Bombay City in 1929 and 1932*, 24 November 1936, in File No. 870 (14) (Maharashtra State Archives, Presidency College, Bombay).

May says that the causes of the riot are obscure.[18] One cause appears to be found in the refusal of Hindus to contribute alms for the Muharram procession while another is that a Muslim boy struck a cow. A second theme in the official accounts of the 1932 riots is of how the civil disobedience movement against colonial authorities turns communal. The Press note quotes from a local Congress pamphlet: "The Congress had been trying to ensure that a large turbulent crowd would gather at Wadala in order to break into the [salt] works and steal and deface the factory." Posters had been pasted all over the city stating that "All roads lead to Wadala." Following strong police presence at Wadala, the crowd, with characteristic proletarian thrift, turns its ire on Muslims, who then retaliate. The Press note is clear. The civil disobedience movement threatens Muslims more than it does colonial authorities.

Riot traces: Outbreak and the Contagion

From reading the reports to the Government of India and Press Communiqués issued by the Director of Information the riot is formulated through a series of statements. These statements are important not because they allow us to analyze the relationship between the author and what he says, but because they establish how Hindu-Muslim violence can be meaningfully understood. Written in the third person, these statements conceal the subjectivity of the writer. But they also make the riot occur in language, as a set of formal characteristics by which it becomes impossible to assign collective responsibility for the violence. These formal characteristics can, however, be registered through their linguistic traces.

Schematically, these traces are first developed in the 1894 report. When it talks of crowds and criminals, of the distribution of the riot over the native city, of intra-class warfare (between Hindu mill hands against Muslim mobs who issue from the Jama Masjid), the *Report* marks a polemical engagement within native society – the primordial antagonism between Hindus and Muslims. Controlling the riot becomes a mode of addressing the inequalities of native soci-

---

[18] *Home Department (Special), Hindu-Mohammadan Riots in Bombay City, May 1932 Reports to the Government of India and Press Communiqués issued by the Director of Information*, in File No. 793 (Maharashtra State Archives, Presidency College, Bombay).

ety within Bombay. The riot itself is pregnant with the future. Among the various causes that embitter Hindu-Muslim relations is the 'greater forwardness of the Hindus in the race of life and their more active participation in the spirit and practice of modern organisation.'[19] The consequent exclusion of Muslims will further estrange them from Hindus. As for Hindus, advanced ideas introduced by western education will produce also a 'Hindu revival.' Its marked features "are the active propagandism carried out by itinerant religious preachers, and the development of the societies for the protection of kin."[20] The riot becomes indexical but in a way that it is addressed in terms of administrative and legal criteria, not as political expression marking the birth of new social actors.[21] Through the riot a future is set in play (of progress and revival within Hindu society and continued sullen resentment within Muslim society), while Hindu-Muslim relations are located within a historical tradition of animosity.

The 1929 report and the documents detailing the 1932 riot develop one or other of the themes laid out in the 1894 report. The 1929 report plays on the theme of intra-class warfare that turns communal, a theme that will resonate repeatedly. "Experience shows that in India riots are apt to take a communal turn."[22] It recommends that "Government should take drastic action against the activities of communists in Bombay."[23] Yet 'poorer classes' rarely enter into communal strife. Such violence is the handiwork of agitators who 'stir up' trouble and who are the contagion.[24] Therefore during a riot hooligans must be arrested or expelled from the city. In conflating the riot with the hooligan menace the 1929 report privileges the

---

[19] George Russell, *East India (Religious Disturbances): Copies or Extracts of Reports Relating to the Recent Conflicts between Hindu and Muhammadans in India, and particularly to the Causes which led To them*, (London: Eyre and Spottiswoode, 1894), 59.

[20] Ibid., 60.

[21] The elaboration of a riot prevention scheme (1931), the experimental use of tear gas on rioters, corporal punishment, including whipping, the banning of kirpans, (swords) are ways of restoring order.

[22] *Home Department (Special), Report of the Bombay Riots Inquiry Committee 1929*, 9, in File No. 543 (10) (E) (B), (Maharashtra State Archives, Presidency College, Bombay).

[23] Ibid., 79.

[24] Ibid., 76-77.

agency of those it thinks are most likely to initiate violence. In the process, this report substantiates the views of the 1894 report. First formulated in the 1894 report the concept of criminal classes and its synonyms, the hooligan or the *mawali*, are permanently occupied by the colonial archive after 1929. The efficacy of this classification establishes a boundary, a condition of possibility determining a capacity to act as well as circumscribing this action. In determining how to act this typology constitutes an administrative agency.[25]

Consider for a moment two tracts produced after the 1928 riot – *Instructions for the Guidance of Honorary Presidency Magistrates* (1929) and resolution number 8385 (10 August 1931) in the form of a memorandum elaborating a riot prevention scheme. The *Instructions* state that a magistrate on duty with the military during times of disturbance represents the civil power of the government. It is his duty to decide when force should be used, in his power to prohibit unlawful assembly (Section 141 of the Indian Penal Code) and call on a military officer to quell a riot. But the procedures used to quell a riot depend on the discretion of the military officer and the magistrate has no power to direct a particular form of force. Thus the riot occurs within zones delimited by the magistrate at hand and his power is made effective in terms of these zones. The assumption is that there is a correspondence between the *Instructions* and what is understood as a riot.[26]

If the *Instructions* delimit the powers of the magistrate during a riot, the riot prevention scheme (*Memorandum 8385*) attempts to generalize the prevention of communal strife.[27] While preventive measures are best suited to particular circumstances, the riot prevention scheme speaks with the weight of experience. Prevention is formulated in three stages – controlling the building of tensions,

---

[25] By agency I refer to an economy of action, one that does not coincide with individual bodies. Administrative agency is circumscribed by law but also has the power to institute particular tasks. This action is also representative to the extent that actions are carried out in the name of the Crown. For a discussion on agency see Talal Asad, *Formations of the Secular: Christianity, Islam, Modernity,* (Stanford, California: Stanford University Press, 2003), 67-99.

[26] *Instructions for the Guidance of Honorary Presidency Magistrates on duty with Military Detachments in times of disturbance in Bombay City* (Bombay: Bombay Central Press, 1929)

[27] Resolution No. 8385: Prevention of and measures for bringing disorder, when they occur, under control, Government of Bombay, Political Department 1931.

procedures to quell outbreaks, instituting punitive and rehabilitation measures after a riot. In the memorandum it is clear that the three stages of the riot are integrated into the functions of governmentality. Here, "early and continuous information [of the riot] is necessary, even although the circumstances may be such as to render it unnecessary or even undesirable for the local officers to intervene in the early stages."[28] The principles of governmentality are directed by forming "conciliation boards for the amicable adjustment of religious and social disputes."[29] These boards are not an external criterion of sovereign decision – they are vitally tied to maintaining order. Accordingly, precautionary measures are proposed, such as banning procession during times of tension, keeping continuous vigil, increasing police pickets and establishing efficient means of communication.

Most importantly, the riot prevention scheme establishes the temporality of the riot – a linear sequence that will henceforth be written as causes, outbreaks and commissions of enquiry. From 1932 onwards riots will be ordered into phases and they will be located within the semantics of causality. What was written of in 1894 as an almost spontaneous eruption over the native city is now placed in sequence and made available for administrative fiat.

Riot and Disease

Yet, underlying the phasing of the riot into stages is the power of repetition. Having accepted the riot as an administrative problem, its writing in postcolonial India is informed by the same structure – cause, outbreak and commission of enquiry. At the heart of this structure we find a predicative judgment that thinks of and constitutes violence as a disease of epidemic proportions. The 1894 report argues that the 11 August outbreak could not have been prevented. "[T]here were irritating causes at work which rendered an eruption inevitable."[30] The main cause of the outbreak is "the infection spread by the riots which had broken out in other parts of India especially those at Prabhas Patan [a district in neighboring Gujarat], and the uneasy feeling generated through them among Muham-

---

[28] Ibid., 2.
[29] Ibid., 3.
[30] George Russell, *East India (Religious Disturbances)*, 23.

madans that Muhammadanism and the followers of that faith generally were suffering at the hands of the Hindus."[31] The agents of such
eruption are the Musalman ruffians, called Chilli Chors engaged in
the occupation of driving small bullock carts. Together with the Ju-
lais (weavers from Hindustan, not a few of whom are Wahabis),
these hooligans function as a contagion, infecting all those who come
in their way.[32] The 1929 report recommends "the institution of a settlement up-country for the Bombay hooligans, on the lines of the
provision in force in England, in order that Bombay may get rid of
them, and that they may have an opportunity of doing some useful
work."[33]

The threat of the contagion is extended to the immigrant to
the city. Act No XIV of 1938 amends the Police Act of 1902,[34] by
which the police are able to deal with people who are a danger to the
city. Section 27 of the City of Bombay Police Act, 1902 states that
whenever it appears to the Commissioner of Police that a body of
persons in the city are causing or are liable to "cause danger or
alarm, or a reasonable suspicion that unlawful designs are enter-
tained by such gang or body,... or that an outbreak of epidemic diseases is likely to result from the continued residence in the City of
large number of pauper-immigrants," he may direct such members to
remove themselves from the city.[35] The amended Act of 1938 formal-
izes and places side-by-side the threat posed by the riot and the epidemic. Those that threaten order are gangs of people whose
movements cause alarm, those who are carriers of epidemic diseases
and crowds who are gathered for unlawful assembly. In such instances the Provincial Government may declare the proclamation of
an emergency. Section 23 of the Bombay Police Act, IV of 1902 is
invoked to spatialize the emergency. The carrying of weapons in public places is prohibited and curfew orders are promulgated over the

---

[31] Ibid., 25.
[32] Ibid., 30.
[33] *Home Department (Special) Report of the Bombay Riots Inquiry Committee 1929,* 9, in File No. 543 (10) (E) (B), (Maharashtra State Archives, Presidency College, Bombay).
[34] Bombay Government Gazette, 10 June 1938, (1) Acts of the Local Legislature of the Bombay Presidency and (2) Acts of the Indian Legislature Assented to by the Governor General.
[35] Ibid.

'affected' areas. These pronouncements are made in the *Bombay Government Gazette*. These orders extend over the native city. A notification of 16 October 1936 mentions and names the affected areas, about ninety in all. Presumably European colonies are not threatened by this contagion. The *Bombay Presidency Weekly Letter* of 31 October 1936 localizes the disease:

> During the recent riots in Bombay [Byculla Temple-Mosque Dispute] there was always the possibility that the communal virus might spread to districts in the Presidency even though on former similar occasions no such tendency had been noticed…If further proof is needed, it is here furnished that India thinks very parochially and that its people can be made only with great difficulty to interest themselves in any matter which is not primarily one of local and direct personal interest.[36]

The idea that the riot is a disease finds mention also in nationalist reportage. For instance, *The Bombay Congress Bulletin* of 17 May 1932 states, 'Blood-lust which descended on Bombay on Saturday evening like a plague has not lifted yet on Tuesday dawn. Murder stalks the streets while Loot and Arson, Fright and Terror make up his ghastly train. Each passing hour piles tragedy on tragedy. And perched on that bloody eminence the *Mawali* is still king in the gullies of Central Bombay.'[37]

In both accounts, the struggle for understanding the riot is formulated through the concept of disease. This concept fixes the riot and then shows how the latter is distributed over the city. The force exerted by the disease is thought to be external to reason. Colonial documents hold that this force does not originate in the relation between the colonial state and native society, but is characteristic of an unthinking mass, incapable of rational discussion. The *Congress Bul-*

---

[36] *Home Department (Special) Extract from the Bombay Presidency Weekly Letter no. 44*, 31 October 1936, in File No. 870 (14) 9 (Maharashtra State Archives, Presidency College, Bombay).

[37] *Home Department (Special) Civil Disobedience Movement May 1932*, Bombay City Reports, in File No. 872 (72) Pt. 4 (Maharashtra State Archives, Presidency College, Bombay).

letin argues that the riot emerges from manipulated colonial subjects whose violence will invite greater state intervention. In fact the *Bulletin* demands such intervention. In either case, the riot as disease is staged publicly. Here the disease is pure physical force, it communicates nothing except its own savagery. It produces effects through the force of its weight. The words for which the disease is a metonym – plague, infection, virus – are words that have a material force built into them, not words that constitute communicative action in the rational sense. Henceforth, one of the basic features of colonial administration in Bombay will be a constant need to redefine who is a member of the city and who must be removed to its boundaries. Once the diseased-violent pauper immigrant crosses over to the city, colonial administration takes pains to redraw what and who is inside and outside. The case of Bhupal Bharma Pandit is instructive.[38] A resident of Jayasingpur in Kolhapur State and thus a foreigner in British India, Bhupal Pandit prints and distributes nearly ten thousand handbills in Hindi and Gujarati in October 1936 during the Byculla Temple-Mosque riot. The subject of these handbills is the marriage of a Jain boy with a Muslim girl.[39] Following Muslim complaints, Pandit is arrested in October 1936 under Section 3 of the Foreigners Act and deported to Kolhapur State. The Police Commissioner prepares a statement regarding Bhupal Pandit that marks out in forensic detail the criminal history of the offender.

Imprinted on this sheet (see Table 1) is an image of Pandit's history and its alignment to space. The function of this sheet is that it both describes the legacy of an individual's criminality, and plays a remedial role in rectifying the wrongs inflicted by similarly situated individuals. Implicitly this sheet relies on the view that the office of

---

[38] *Home Department (Special), (1) Proposal to deal with one Abdalla H.Kermali under Section 3 and 4 of the Bombay (Special) Emergency Powers Act 1932 in connection with Agitation over Byculla Temple Sabha Mandap Reconstruction. (2) Deportation of Bhupal Bharma Pandit under the Foreigners Act 1864,* 17 October 1936, in File No. 870 (10) 1936 (Maharashtra State Archives, Presidency College, Bombay).

[39] The handbill is worded thus: "One thing is accomplished. My brother, Shripad Jhas, has brought the Hindu society, the Muslim society and the Jain religion together by marrying a Muslim sister Ashabi. And many such true events have taken place and are taking place. Hence what benefit will be reaped by quarrelling among yourselves in connection with a temple or a mosque? There is no benefit indeed: the truth is the same in your Kuran and Puranas."

the Police Commissioner has the power to regulate the boundaries of an individual's assimilation into the city. This logic makes the right to remedy historically contingent. Furthermore, characterizing Bhupal Pandit in this way is a function of government agencies, such as the police. This function transforms lives of criminals into cases, taking away from their stories the making of these circumstances. Foucault describes the power of the biographical account as not a 'monument for future memory,' but a document for possible use. "This turningofreal lives into writing is no longer a procedure of heroization; it functions as a procedure for objectification and subjectification."[40]

Description	Caste: Hindu, Religion Or Nationality; Digambar Jain Age: 24 years, Height: 5 ft. 6 in. Complexion: Sallow, Build: Medium Identification Marks: Two cut Marks – one on Forehead and the other on chin
Name & Subject	Village: Jayasingpur, Kolhapur State
Arrival In British India	1932
Residence In Bombay	Liberty Liking Tailoring Home, Kamathi Building, Opposite Plaza Cinema, Lady Jamshedji Road, Dadar
Whether In Possession of Passport	--------------------------

---

[40] Michel Foucault, *Discipline and Punish: The Birth of the Prison,* trans. Alan Sheridan (England: Penguin Books, 1977), 191-92.

Remarks	1) Convicted and sentenced to be sent to Dharwar Borstal (Reformatory) School by First Class Magistrate, Bandra under Section 17(i) of the Criminal Law Amendment Act of 25.4.32 (under the name of Ganpat Tukaram More) 2) Convicted and sentenced to four months rigorous imprisonment by First Class Magistrate, Bandra, under Section 7(b) of the Criminal Law Amendment Act of 22.3.34

Table 1

Sd. J. W. Rowland Commissioner of Police, Bombay, 24 October 1936.
Source: File 870(10) Home Department (Special), 1936 Bombay Archives,
Elphinston College

In post colonial India the infection initiated by the riot is noted in various commissions of enquiry but now a second and disquieting element is introduced – the idea that the state itself is infected with communalism, seen in its partisan handling of violence. To see the resilience of the concept of the disease and its distribution over the city I will now look at the *Report of the Srikrishna Commission*.

The Srikrishna Commission

On 25 January 1993 the Government of Maharashtra constituted the Srikrishna Commission to inquire into the circumstances, events and immediate causes of the violence that occurred in the Bombay Police Commissionerate area and to affix responsibility for the violence. The Commission was also charged with determining the adequacy of preventive measures undertaken by the police to quell the violence. The evidence of the involvement of the Shiv Sena and other political parties of the right, of police bias against Muslims, forced the government to demonstrate its commitment to justice.[41] It did this by investing the Commission, headed by the High Court judge, Justice Srikrishna, with the dignity of legitimacy. Although the findings of the Commission were not legally binding upon the gov-

---

[41] Thomas Blom Hansen, *Wages of Violence: Naming and Identity in Postcolonial Bombay* (Princeton: Princeton University Press, 2001), 38.

ernment, the Commission functioned as a legal body.[42] It decided to make the proceedings public and to call upon a number of interested parties to let themselves be represented through legal counsel along with the Commission's legal advocate. The Shiv Sena-BJP government in Maharashtra, in power when the Report was prepared, delayed its release. The SCR appeared in August 1998, five and a half years after the riot. It was left to the state government to decide whether the evidence could be used to institute criminal prosecutions.

When the Shiv Sena assumed office in 1995 the principal area of conflict between the government and the Commission related to the release of various documents and files. In some cases the Advocate General refused to release the files on the basis of 'interest of state,' but the state could not in principle claim privilege and refuse to hand over the files (according to the *Commissions of Inquiry Act*). On 23rd January 1996 the state government of Maharashtra dissolved the Srikrishna Commission, but five months later, following pressure from the central government, it restored the Commission, though with a changed mandate. The Commission would include the bomb blasts of March 1993 to arrive at a formula of balanced and equally apportioned guilt.

In the eyes of the Commission, this violence is irrational and perhaps incurable. "For five days in December 1992 (6-10 December) and fifteen days in January 1993 (6-20 January), Bombay, prima urbs of this country was rocked by riots and violence unprecedented in magnitude and ferocity, as though the forces of Satan were let loose, destroying all human values and civilized behaviour."[43] The opening sentence frames violence in cataclysmic terms and later as a chronic disease. "Communal riots...are like incurable epileptic seizures, whose symptoms, though dormant over a period of time,

---

[42] According to the Commissions of Inquiry Act, 1952, any proceeding before a commission of inquiry is a judicial proceeding 'within the meaning of sections 193 and 228 of the Indian penal Code (45 of 1860)', as cited in Hanson, *Wages of Violence*, 5). The commission functions like a civil court and can summon persons and documents.

[43] Hon. Justice Srikrishna, *Report of the Srikrishna Commission Appointed for Inquiry into the Riots at Mumbai During December 1992 and January 1993*. (Vol. I & II, published privately by Jyoti Punwani and Vrijendra. 1998), 1.

manifest themselves over and over again."[44] Later the SCR will talk of a 'communal virus.' Violence so designated is an aberration. It must be explained through formal procedures of accountability, the *raison d'être* of the Commission. In the SCR the conflation of disease and violence establishes solidarity with colonial records of the riot. In exploring the breakdown of public security, the Commission divides the riot into five phases: the build up to the riot, the period from 6 to 12 December 1992, the period from 12 December 1992 to 5 January 1993, the phase from 6 January to 20 January, the period subsequent to 20 January 1993. As with colonial records, the riot is put into phases and discussed through episodes. It has a well-established temporality and a force of its own that is distributed over the city. The agents of violence are of course 'mobs,' 'crowds' and above all 'criminals,' instigated by Muslim 'fanatics' and political parties.

In dealing with the attack on the legitimate authority of the state and the restoration of law, the SCR invests such legitimacy with dignity. Rather than seeing the SCR and the TADA courts as state spectacles of impartial and universal justice leading to public catharsis[45] I read the Report in two ways. First, it indicates the dual character of political power. Second, it does this by employing certain discursive practices.[46]

As far as the first point is concerned it is clear that for Srikrishna the riot is not within the remit of power, it is rather that a particular (illegitimate) power has issued from the riot which allows him to identify relations of violence between protagonists. Their modes of

---

[44] Ibid., 4.

[45] Thomas Blom Hansen, *Wages of Violence: Naming and Identity in Postcolonial Bombay* (Princeton: Princeton University Press, 2001), 48-49.

[46] Kantorowicz shows that the dual character of political power rests on the notion of dignity embodied in the figure of the king. The king has two bodies, one that is the law, a sacred eternal body, and the other that is a human body. However, when society cannot be represented as a unified body or be embodied in the figure of the king, the nation state takes the place of the king in terms of the principle of dignity and functions within the terrain of law. My attempt is not to trace the emergence of the modern state. I follow Agamben's (*Homo Sacer: Sovereign Power and the Bare Life.* Trans. Daniel Heller-Roazen. Stanford, California: Stanford University Press, 1998: 91-111) discussion of Kantorowicz (*The King's Two Bodies.* Princeton: Princeton University Press, 1957) to show that dignity is emancipated from its bearer, in particular how dignity is embodied in the state and in those individuals who, following communal violence, make claims on the state.

actions challenge public authority so as to invite counter-measures from the police and concerned civil groups. Here, the riot becomes the terrain where the division between the sphere of the state and that of civil society tends to blur. But Srikrishna also holds that power is symbolic, that it designates an empty place that no one can seize. The SCR locates itself within a juridical codification of political power and argues that agencies of the state – particularly the police – have been unable to uphold the dignity of law. While the technical means of controlling the riot are linked to the exercise of disciplinary power as framed in law, procedures of redress disqualify, at least implicitly, a rationality based solely on police techniques. In arguing for redress and rehabilitation the SCR does not threaten sovereignty. It merely identifies that society has to be governed according to law. The riot puts society into crisis and the signs of this are seen in the inability of the police to enforce preventive measures, the failure of the intelligence apparatuses to maintain a list of communal hooligans and the inadequacy of registering riot related offences.[47] The SCR seeks to restore the efficacy of the democratic system by an administrative recording of violence and its causes and a simultaneous critique of what it calls Hindu communal politics and the police force in Bombay. In this way it hopes to restore dignity to legitimacy.

This legitimacy, however, is not purely juridical - it must take recourse to morality. The SCR reveals the appalling inefficiency of policing and a distinct bias against Muslims, of the bald attempts of the Shiv Sena-BJP government to obstruct the proceedings of the Commission. Srikrishna details the complicity of the police in the riots in pessimistic terms. "Despite knowledge of the fact that the force had been infected by communal virus, no effective curative steps were taken over a large period of time as a result of which communal violence became chronic and its virulent symptoms showed up during the two riot periods."[48] The Commission stands for the perpetuity of a higher form of justice. "That vicious communal violence on such scale should occur in the land of ... Mahatma Gandhi, only shows that the message of love and brotherhood

---

[47] Hon. Justice Srikrishna, *Report of the Srikrishna Commission Appointed for Inquiry into the Riots at Mumbai During December 1992 and January 1993*, (Vol. I & II, published privately by Jyoti Punwani and Vrijendra, 1998), 30-32.
[48] Ibid., 35.

preached by apostles is not internalized. Unless this is done the spectre of communal violence would haunt the city again and again."[49] It is this idea of the state as a moral entity that is at once the most sublime and the most unattainable.

The SCR employs two discursive strategies to order the riot. It places the violence within a defined and given period, and a given geographic area. The spatial and temporal ordering imposed on the violence and its convergence with particular institutions and practices leads to the discourse of the riot. This discourse is folded within the colonial archive. As with colonial records the SCR characterizes violence in the language of disease. This report thinks of the riot as a pathological object that must be recorded, its causes determined and remedies suggested. Accordingly, it details the 'build up' (pp. 5-8) to the violence, noting the perfidy of minority appeasement and the vicious reaction of Hindu political parties, of judicial delays and failure of various central governments in arriving at amicable solutions to the Hindu-Muslim problem. The SCR then describes the 'immediate causes' (pp. 25-27) of the violence, observing that an economic or class dimension to the violence cannot be sustained, though the processes by which the labour force has been pushed into the informal sector makes such people especially vulnerable to communal aggression. The ghettoizing of Muslims in distinct areas of the city allied with a changing political discourse has led to a hardening of boundaries, social and spatial, between Hindus and Muslims.

In a second sense the SCR sees the riot as pointing toward the pressure of time. In locating the riot within a temporality – 6 December 1992 to 20 January 1993 (pp. 12-25) – the SCR hopes to stabilize the ruling order through legal preservation or legal finding. To the spatial meaning of the riot the SCR adds a historical unfolding. "The sense of camaraderie, which existed between the Hindus and the Muslims when they were united in their efforts to throw the British out of this country, appeared to have vaporized and vanished with the 'two Nation theory' advocated by Mohammed Ali Jinnah." In this sense the riot is another constellation of power beginning with the rise of communalism. Here the riot indicates the crossing of a

---

[49] Ibid.

threshold, a process that repeats itself over and over again. The riot is an iterative concept with a well-established periodicity.

What, then, are the discursive practices by which the dignity of legitimacy is put in place? These practices spatialize the riot by alphabetizing the city in terms of neighbourhoods. Second, they assign a precise chronology to the violence. Third, they document the testimonies of various named actors in the riots. Through these practices the riot is ordered, but it is important to recognize that this ordering is drawn from an archive of communal violence. As with colonial records the riot is seen as a public contest. More appropriately, for the SCR the history of this violence is made visible on city spaces in Bombay and as this history becomes visible the riot is treated as revelatory: a repository of the relations between Hindus and Muslims. The reference to past violence (Bhiwandi, the partition) with its allegories of fragmentation and ruin inform Justice Srikrishna's monument to public remembrance. As with colonial enquiry committee reports, the riot is placed in linear time, spatialized in neighbourhoods and framed within causality. The SCR allows for individual testimony only to the extent that different individuals substantiate this ordering.

The ordering of the riot through depositions, affidavits, testimonies, eyewitness accounts and so on follows the method undertaken by colonial reports – the attempt to understand the riot as pathology. The SCR, it is true, does not add or subtract to our understanding of medical discourse, but it records the riot as if it were a disease, first initiated in the 1894 report. As with the 1929 report, it surveys the distribution of violence, marks its onset and development (colonial records ascertain this disturbance on a daily basis as is evident in the reports of various commissioners of police) and the transformations that it undergoes. This mapping of violence does not have to pass through speaking subjects – in fact the riot is much more than individual speech. It has its own configuration and its own historicity, drawing from the method of writing earlier instances of Hindu-Muslim violence. The problem with violence, thus, is not merely one of behaviour. It is linked to the consolidation of meaning – in this case the mapping of disease.

This mapping is a kind of discursive practice by which designated spaces acquire meaning only to the extent that they threaten order. The SCR, then, is part of an archive in the sense of Foucault.[50] The archive coordinates and subordinates subject positions in which the riot appears and is defined. Subject positions are designated historically and in this designation time is distributed – the riot is segmented into periods and given a regular chronology. Thus, the archive of the riot, of which the SCR is part, authors a set of discursive statements that cause a multiplicity of violent practices to emerge as regular events.

Testimony, Remembrance and Everyday Life

If the SCR attempts to re-dignify the legitimacy of the state, individual testimonies of violence bear witness to the stripping away of dignity. And if the archive establishes a referential relation between violence and language, testimony strives to speak the unsayable, with all its attendant ellipses and necessary forgetting. In the archive the subject is an empty position, generalizable and framed within the already written. In testimony, the position of the subject is unique and non-reproducible. Testimony's bid for presence depends on the capacity for recall of remembered events, but a recall that is always coloured by perjury and forgetfulness.

Against the discourse of the SCR, which exhausts the meaning of the riot so that objects of reform can be proposed, testimony treats the riot as lived experience. This suggests that it is in everyday life that violence as an experience of particularly dramatic moments of subjectivity is authored and translated. Once translated, it loses its exceptional character and becomes a 'normal' and banal phenomenon. When placed in the quotidian it is almost as if violence is a singular mode of apprehending immediate agonies. In this sense, violence mentioned in the testimonies is not systematized but is prosaic – a fact of one's existence, belonging to the realm of the obvious and yet always coloured by irony. Second, violence is seldom subject to a stable analysis. Since 1994, when I started fieldwork in Dharavi, I have found that descriptions of violence have changed. This change is consistent with a shared ensemble of a reconfigured everyday life, most evident in the changed topography of the slum. If in 1994 and

---

[50] Michel Foucault, *The Archaeology of Knowledge*, trans. Alan Sheridan (New York: Pantheon Books, 1972), 128-32.

1995 descriptions of violence showed how national boundaries were played out in the slum, in 1999 and 2000 the same violence was linked to the construction of high-rise buildings in Dharavi and the allotment of apartments to residents. Violence was now the product of the ruses of venal politicians, bureaucracies and builders. In 2003 and 2004 we found that the violence of 1992-93 had congealed in at least two different ways. In the first instance this violence now belonged firmly to the past – one could not draw more lessons from it than had already been learnt and in any case there was no reason to remind oneself of those days. As one of our informants mockingly said, 'When we have to remind ourselves we will come to you.' But in a second sense 1992-93 had left behind a residue of fear that continued to direct one's relationships with one's neighbours, especially if they belonged to an opposing religious group.

Given this fear and forgetfulness what can be the relation of the speech of the testifier to the event to which the testifier claims to bear witness? Can we find traces of the archive playing itself out in such speech?[51] I will present the testimony of one resident, called Ali (pseudonym) of Dharavi. His experiences of violence have often colored our interactions with others in Dharavi, continuing to inform their narratives. Insofar as Ali's story touches on a memory of loss, the refusal to forget and its consequences, of police violence and its corrupting influence, this account is perhaps indexical of how violence was represented to us in 1994 and 1995. And yet, going over what others said, this story is different. Ali's concern is not so much to detail the intricacies of the violence, as it is to focus on its effects.

We met Ali in October 1999. He is in his late fifties and lives in one of the many chawls of Dharavi. He was a leather worker who has now become a prosperous landlord, waiting to shift into one of the many high-rise apartment blocks that dot the slum. Ali came to

---

[51] Even in the case of those who have pushed the events of 1992-93 into the past we find that violence though distanced in time is experienced as spatially contemporaneous. Certain neighborhoods and high-rise apartments are marked as being produced by the violence of 1992-93, certain neighbours, who participated in the violence, are evoked in a way that 1992-93 becomes the defining feature of their biography. Simultaneously, the violence of 1992-93 is compared with earlier and later events of Hindu-Muslim warfare (Bhiwandi in 1984, Gujarat in 2002). Violence is thus placed within historical time and it is perhaps here that the archive impresses itself on the testifier.

Bombay from Aligarh in the 1960s and shifted to Dharavi in the next decade. He is married and has four living sons and two daughters. Ali was, until the last year, an active member of the *Tablighi Jamaat*, an Islamist organization. He says that in Aligarh he was first introduced to the Deobandi School of Islamic persuasion, but later joined the *Tablighis* in Bombay after the 1992 riots.

In 1994 when I first visited Dharavi I heard that Ali had suffered an especially bad fate during the riots. I made repeated requests to meet him, but Ali was never available. A year later we again made attempts to meet him. After one such effort, we were told to let it be; perhaps Ali did not want to talk. Then in 1999 Ali came of his own accord and spoke to us. The conversation occurred over more than two hours in the office of an NGO called PROUD. There were seven people present in the meeting.

> Ali: It (the violence) happened because of the masjid, but before it was broken the environment had become bad. What were we to know? We saw their rallies...I had gone to work that day (6 December 1992, the day the masjid fell). In the evening I heard the news... It started the next day at eleven in the morning with stones and continued for seven days until the 14th. On 8th December my son was martyred, Iftikar was his name (larka shaheed hua, Iftikar uska nam tha). It happened across the [Joglekar] nullah (drain). Allauddin told me his body was lying on the other side. I got him back here; he had been shot in the head...what could I do? Outside was curfew...His body was on the bed for three days. Together with a policeman I took the maiyyat (corpse that has passed through the hands of women) to the police station. They said that they were sending the body for post-mortem to the Rajabari hospital. I pleaded for his body to be removed to the JJ hospital. I knew what they would do in their hospital. They would turn him into another criminal. When I kept on pleading the police said, "Should we send you to Pakistan, too?" [laughs]. With the help of Dattu Khatke [a councilor during the riots of 1992 and a member of the Shiv Sena] I had the post-mortem done in JJ hospital. I went in curfew and came in curfew.

The ironies of this account are immediately apparent. Ali takes his son's body to the police station with the help of a policeman, presumably a member of a force that is in Ali's eyes responsible for his son's death – the politics over the post-mortem and Ali's ironic laughter over the statement of the police confirms this. It requires the intercession of a member of a political party, whose role in the violence is well documented, for Ali to take his son's body to JJ hospital. Perhaps, it is only in the ironic mode that Ali is able to constitute his subjectivity. The actuality of violence is either forgotten or rationalized. But his irony is threatened by loss. His subsequent statements point in this direction.

In answer to the question of what happened after Iftiqar's death, he says,

> What happened? They made me naked. I filled in forms and gave evidence so that his death would not go unrecorded. I went to the hospital. You see my hands? They tremble...the effect of the masjid is still there. The masjid politicians have all benefited from this hatred, all are complicit. But has fate decreed that not one believer be present in these parties?
> Q: Where did you give evidence?
> Ali: I went to the Krishna Commission. It recommended my name because I had the post-mortem result. My son's death must be recorded. [Touching me] You don't understand. I don't want their money. My son's death must be recorded .

Here the past is not closed, but acts upon Ali's present and is perhaps actualized in the present. This actuality is of a kind where Iftikar's death does not enter the flow of time as continuity between past, present and future. It is almost as if past and present merge in the relationship of caring that Ali enters into with his dead son. He asks me, "Can you understand what happened?" Such rhetorical assertions are the performative statements of those who are marked by the inescapable presence of violence and are also uttered as a means of incorporating their pain into the care-structure of a larger humanity. In contrast, in the SCR the testimony of various participants in the violence will be fully realized only in the future, when the objects of reform proposed by it achieve fruition. The Report is not concerned with the present moment of testimony, with the pathos and anger that runs through the accounts. Nor is it concerned with how individuals incorporate this violence in their daily lives.

With the grace of God I've recovered. This year [1999] I went on my second Haj (pilgrimage to Mecca). I went with the delegation of the Jamaat. I went for the first time last year. People now call me a Haji [laughs]. After my son's martyrdom they called me mad. The mad person is now a Haji [laughs].

After the conversation, we were told that Ali was on medical treatment. It is not merely his son's death that hastens his illness, but as he tells it, his illness is placed side-by-side with the effects of the demolition of the mosque and the corrupt practices of political parties. It would be tempting to read the resolution of Ali's loss in his immersion in the various practices of the Jama'at. It is almost as if the pilgrimage to Mecca fills in the void of his son's death. His use of the term *Shaheed* suggests this. But to read it in this way is to argue that his loss engenders a re-moralizing of the self. It cannot account for his ironic laughter. If we are to take his irony seriously then we must recognize that Ali is able to locate his son's death in language and to articulate through this death his version of a permitted past. What silences his irony is not a theological guarantee but an equivocation that comes from his negotiation with the state.

Q: Has communal hatred become less now?
Ali: How is that possible? How can we forget...?
Aslam: He's asking if Hindus and Muslims fight. They don't. The situation in 1992-93 was different. In those days...
Ali: No, he's asking if there's hatred. Of course there is. The Krishna report is there. It names people. Until they are punished you can forget about living peacefully.
Q: Weren't those responsible for your son's death punished?
Ali: I admit it. I got compensation. You don't understand. I'm still able-bodied and I can earn with my hands, even if they tremble. The state (*sarkar*) gave me money. It apologized for his death. With the sarkar it's about profit and loss. The police take and the officer gives. Every time after a *danga* we fill 'applications' [for compensation]. It happened after Bhiwandi [early 1984] and it happened after the *danga*. The history of 'Akhand Bharat' is found in applications (*Akhand Bharat ka itihas applications men mile ga*).

Rhetorically, this account indicates a stylized conversation with the motive of reprobation – a dramatic representation of wrong and its redress. Apart from its rhetorical foundation Ali's version points to the politics of memory. This politics refers to the process by which an accumulated and shared historical experience of communal conflict constrains today's political action. It shows the contest over the proper interpretation of that historical experience. For Ali this experience is found in a dual understanding of the state. In the first instance, the state is the agency through which brutal violence is perpetrated, and in the second, it redefines such violence through bureaucratic procedure. His understanding is close to that generated by the SCR, which dignifies legitimacy by domesticating violence. If the SCR acknowledges the complicity of the police in the violence, it also recommends cases for rehabilitation. Ali is compensated for his son's death: he is given a sum of fifty thousand rupees by the state government. It is assumed that cases like Ali's will reach closure once they are rehabilitated. In a second sense, however, violence is mobilized through a form of remembrance that is transported through the iconography of the body. It is not only his son's body that lies in his house for three days, but Ali himself evokes violence as a corporeal memory – his madness and trembling fingers, together with his verbal discourse produce the effects of violence. This memory – of the body and in speech – of violence is a kind of phantasm, outside of public documents and of history. From the point of view of the testifier this memory is a kind of haunting.[52]

I met Ali again in September 2004. He has become a prosperous businessman, having invested his money in the new apartments that are being built in Dharavi. In December 2003 he hired a shop in south Bombay to sell leather shoes and slippers, but gave up the business when the landlord of the shop insisted on raising the rent. Ali is no longer a member of the Tablighi Jama'at but continues to remain a pious Muslim. He is now a grandfather and takes care of his daughter's children. His surviving sons are settled in Dharavi, and one of them stays with Ali supplying belts and buckles to various shops in Bombay. He was apparently with Iftikar when the latter was shot in December 1992. Ali divulges this as an aside in the following

---

[52] I take my notion of haunting or 'spectrality' from Derrida (*Specters of Marx: The State of the Debt, the Work of Mourning and the New International*, trans. Peggy Kamuf [New York and London: Routledge, 1994]).

conversation. I was interested in pursuing Ali's success story and asked him whether raising money for his business ventures had been difficult.

> Ali: I had some savings and I used the compensation for my *larka* (boy, meaning Iftikar) with care.
> Q: Compensation?
> Ali: After Iftikar I got money. The Krishna Commission gave me a *parcha* (document).
> Q: Did the Jama'at have anything to say about this?
> Ali: Why should they? Business and Islam aren't strangers. Before you help others you have to be secure. How can I be sure that this will never happen to me again? I don't want to lose Intizar (his son who stays with him). With the grace of God he escaped their guns. I must build my defenses...
> Q: Whose guns?
> Ali: He was a child then, going with the crowds, following Iftikar. Even now I haven't asked him about that day...I must be in a position where when this *danga* happens again, my son doesn't get involved. I have to live here. I also thought that I should use the money for the *quom* (community). But I can't do that by becoming a *fakir* (religious mendicant). I have to take care of my Intizar, my sons, my grandchildren. Nor can you. Do you beg for your child?
> Q: Who do you need to build your defenses against?
> Ali: The situation is bad even now. You think their boys (Shiv Sainiks) are pacified? I make money for my family members, but also for the officers. I gave money for the post-mortem certificate. During their investigations I had to give money for their daily expenses. But that talk is old. I don't wish to become naked again.

This account expresses at least three themes. First for Ali, the public character of the riot follows a pattern of invocation and is located in the social setting of work and home. Both these arenas of everyday life must be made secure from further violence. This security must be formulated vis-à-vis the 'boys' of the Shiv Sena and various agencies of the state. Second, but more than this setting, his experience of the violence of 1992-93 consists in arriving at a mastery of the past. However, this mastery does not assuage his anxiety. He is concerned that his youngest son has been exposed to the unsayable. So long as the effects of violence remain alive his attempt to master the past only makes this violence contemporaneous. Finally, Ali's experience of the violence is necessarily mediated – by the SCR before which he provides evidence, by how he can understand his son's death as martyrdom and in his attempt to build defenses against its repetition.[53] And it is this remembrance that is in the nature of a haunting.

Where do we place Ali's testimony? In a general sense, he is witness to the riots, but also to his son's death. The latter concern is my focus. As survivor, he speaks for him who cannot speak. The SCR, too, speaks in the place of those who lived through the violence, but their speech is always an appendage to the dignity and hopeful impartiality of the state. From the point of view of the SCR the survivor's speech is premised on the factual verification of experience and is located within a long history of communal conflict. Ali mentions that the violence and his subsequent negotiations with the police stripped him of dignity, made him naked. He is able to re-dignify himself, not by successfully having his son's death recorded, nor even by becoming a member of the *Tablighi Jamaat*. His attempt at dignity, precarious and coloured by cynicism, is found in the way he speaks of his son's death as martyrdom and later as a refusal to visit that experience.

Conclusion

In presenting Ali's testimony I have tried to show that his recall of the violence of 1992-93 is mediated by the category of the riot as it has been formulated in official documents. I have tried to emphasize the formation and inheritance of administrative understandings of violence between Hindus and Muslims. In treating the riot as a formative construct the ethnographic data that I have used does not conform to localized settings. The understanding of the riot oscil-

---

[53] The idea of the witness proposed here is contrary to that developed by scholars such as Felman (Shoshana Felman: 'Education and Crisis, or the Vicissitudes of Teaching.' In Shoshana Felman and Dori Laub (eds.) *Testimony: Crisis of Witnessing in Literature, Psychoanalysis and History*, (New York: Routledge, 1992). For Felman, to testify is to produce one's own speech as material evidence for truth. Such speech is performative, a 'discursive practice,' that 'addresses what in history is action,' (*Testimony*, 5). The problem is not of performative speech but of assuming that history moves through the actions of individuals. It may be that for the witness history is experienced as a new temporality and more so when it makes demands on the future.

lates between essential ideas of Hindus and Muslims and their materiality in precise locales and specific performances. We are in the circumscribed space of local groups and residential communities but also within the networks of law and order proposed by the state. Official documents of the riot work with bits and pieces of materiality, rehabilitating old truths in the search for meaning. The riot is a pathology that has specific colonial coordinates. Disease is the root metaphor of the riot and infection and contagion (in the form of the hooligan) make up its body. By the 1930s colonial administrators envision the riot as organic to native society in Bombay and their reports are a kind of diagnostic science of the diseased body of the riot. This vision functions as a genealogical reservoir for the Srikrishna Report. For Srikrishna, colonial modes of analyzing the riot are transposed into the political vernacular of everyday life and positioned as a disease. The formation of the riot is embedded in administrative documents, but is also seen in the accounts of participants in the violence of 1992-93. As witnesses these participants speak of their experiences and also make claims for rehabilitation and compensation. Indeed, it may be that experience and compensation are mutually reinforcing. From the point of view of the SCR testimony reinvigorates the historical project of the riot as disease and a part of it is focused on the containment of infected bodies.

We must, however, also recognize that Ali's testimony (and of others like him) is neither fully accommodated within the archive, nor a mere theatre of language. Ali's account relies on being witness to 1992-93, of being bodily present to his son's death. Part of his testimony is ritualized truth telling and part perhaps confessional. Whatever the truth of his account – we were told that Iftikar was not 'martyred,' that he was discovered and shot by the police while vandalizing a temple during the violence – it is clear that Iftikar's death is lodged not only in bureaucratic efforts of amelioration, but also exists as a shadow in everyday life. Ali's testimony for this reason does not point to a factual truth as much as it moves between what can and cannot be said.

Deepak Mehta *is a Reader in the Department of Sociology, University of Delhi. He is the author of* Work, Ritual, Biography: A Muslim Community in North India *(Delhi: Oxford University Press, 1997).*

Since 1994 he has been researching the Bombay riots of 1992-93 and has published various articles on this subject.

Governmental Technologies & Institutional Practice: NGOs and the Slum-Dwellers' Voice

Roma Chatterji

ABSTRACT

This article seeks to problematize the events that are collectively known as the "Mumbai riots of 1992-93" by establishing an alternative narrative frame that links these events with other events of collective violence that are a ubiquitous feature of everyday life in slum colonies, i.e. demolition of huts. Displacement is a theme that is common to both narratives of communal violence as well as to narratives of slum redevelopment. By foregrounding this theme, the article hopes to establish a connection between different events of collective violence – large-scale demolition drives that invariably accompany governmental projects for slum housing and redevelopment and communal riots. The juxtaposition of these two radically different kinds of events allows us to explore the relationship between violence and everyday life on several different axes. It is also a first step in producing an ethnographic account of state practices and their role in the production of new forms of community. Thus the article describes the process by which governmental technologies such as mapping and enumeration constitute new types of community, by looking at a slum, Dharavi, in Mumbai. NGO activity mediates the relationship between the state and slum dwellers, in the sense that it acts as a catalyst allowing for the emergence of a new identity – that of 'slum dweller' – a member of a 'public' and a community based on common interests as residents in a slum. In the process, however, the self-perception of NGOs, working on slum re-development in Mumbai vis-à-vis the state has now been transformed into one of selective cooperation.

Introduction

I first became interested in slum housing when I heard that the members of a locality that had suffered grievous harm in the Mumbai riots of 1992-93 were thinking of joining a neighbouring *chawl*[1] in proposing a housing project under the government's slum re-habilitation scheme in 1998.[2] This joint venture aroused my curiosity because the 'neighbouring' *chawl* was stereotypically represented as housing some of the worst *taporis* (hooligans)[3] in the area – gang members who were perpetrators of violence in the riots. This seemed to go against the general trend in Mumbai where it was thought that the riots had resulted in residential segregation with Muslims moving out of mixed colonies.[4]

NGOs and Local Slum Communities

Slum housing is one of the significant terrains on which civil society institutions have come to express themselves in Mumbai. It is a site on which state functionaries and non-governmental organizations (henceforth NGO) interact with slum dwellers, leading to the formation of new kinds of communities based on commonality of interest in slum areas.[5] However, as NGOs, often regarded as major players in civil society, come to occupy an increasingly important role in the development process, they are also criticized for indirectly

---

[1] A *chawl* is a segment of a colony, which comprises anything between 130 to 230 single rooms, often with one floor built on top. Sometimes there are as many as three conjugal units that live in one room. See Deepak Mehta & Roma Chatterji, "Boundaries, Names, Alterities: A Case Study of a 'Communal Riot' in Dharavi, Bombay," in Veena Das, Arthur Kleinman, Margaret Lock, Mamphela Ramphele & Pamela Reynolds (eds.), *Remaking the World. Violence, Social Suffering, and Recovery* (Berkeley: University of California Press, 2001), 201-249.
[2] At the time of the 1995 elections in Maharashtra, Balasaheb Thakerey, the Shiv Sena supremo promised that if his party came to power they would ensure that 40 lakh slum dwellers would be re-housed free of cost. The slum re-development scheme that was formulated to execute this promise was popularly known as the *Free Scheme*. An area is officially declared a 'slum,' "Where the Competent Authority is satisfied that - any area is or may be a source of danger to the health, safety or convenience of the public of that area or of its neighbourhood by reason of the area or of its neighbourhood, by reason of the area having inadequate or no basic amenities, or being insanitary, squalid, overcrowded or otherwise" (The Maharashtra Slum Areas (Improvement, Clearance and Redevelopment) Act, 1971, 8601).
[3] 'Tapori' refers to the thin iron rods carried by the young men so designated.
[4] Thomas Blom Hansen, *Wages of Violence: Naming and Violence in Postcolonial Bombay* (New Jersey: Princeton University Press, 2001). See also YUVA, *Planned Segregation. Riots, Evictions and Dispossession in Jogeshwari East* (Mumbai: YUVA Publications, 1996).
[5] Roma Chatterji, "Plans, Habitation and Slum-Redevelopment: The Production of Community in Dharavi, Mumbai." (Delhi: ISERDD Occasional Research Papers Series, 2003).

legitimizing neo-liberal reforms[6] and the new forms of exploitation that follow from this process. Can NGOs still represent the interests of the poor while simultaneously serving as 'delivery systems' for the state as it retreats from its traditional welfare programmes in the wake of neo-liberal reforms (Mendoza and D'Souza 2002)?[7] In this essay I address this question by examining the role of NGOs in the various slum rehabilitation programmes of the state.

What relevance does this have for the understanding of the overall theme of this volume – collective violence and social reconciliation? In a previous work Deepak Mehta and I have argued that emergent events like the Mumbai riots of 1992-93 have the capacity to re-order everyday life.[8] Their effects reverberate through time – re-orienting attitudes to the past and to the future – constituting new subjectivities and new social formations. I argue that a first step in understanding the relationship between communal violence and these changing structures is to examine the discursive formation within which communal violence is articulated. To do this one must abstract this event from the master narrative of the 'communal riot' and map an alternative genealogy that privileges a different temporal

---

[6] This term is used to characterize the process of "destatisization" that is taking place in many countries since the 1980s. As Andrew Lakoff says, "the goal of neoliberal reform was to limit the role of the state in overseeing human welfare, and to extend market rationality to areas that had not previously been seen as economic..." Andrew Lakoff, "The Private Life of Numbers: Pharmaceutical Marketing in Post-Welfare Argentina," *in* Aihwa Ong and Stephen J. Collier (eds.), *Global Assemblages. Technology, Politics, and Ethics as Anthropological Problems* (Malden, MA: Blackwell Publishing, 2005), 194-213.

[7] Walter Mendoza & John D'Souza, *The Long Winding Road. From Structural Change to Structural Transformation* (Mumbai: Centre for Education and Documentation, 2002).

[8] It was the American sociologist GH Mead who posited the notion of the 'emergent event.' Some acts, he said, acquired social significance by 'sticking out' from the flow of time. These acts are emergent events that have the ability to organize time into a past and a future. The event itself remains in the spacious present, acting as a bridge between the two temporal registers of past and future. Hans Joas, *G.H. Mead* (Cambridge: Polity Press, 1985). For our discussion, see Deepak Mehta & Roma Chatterji, "Boundaries, Names, Alterities: A Case Study of a 'Communal Riot' in Dharavi, Bombay" in Veena Das, Arthur Kleinman, Margaret Lock, Mamphela Ramphele & Pamela Reynolds (eds.), *Remaking the World. Violence, Social Suffering, and Recovery* (Berkeley: University of California Press, 2001), 201-249.

pathway.[9] I see this paper as a first step in this process – an exploration of the interface between the state and voluntary organizations in one particular domain, i.e. slum housing. By foregrounding slum housing I hope to show that there are themes that cut across riot narratives in slums to stories about everyday life.

Displacement is one such theme. It is foregrounded in the narratives of the Mumbai riots. There was a perception that the riots had led to some amount of residential polarization. Communities that had been affected by the violence were shifting to 'safer' areas. In recent memory, however, displacement is most often associated with slum demolition especially after the horrific, 2004-2005 demolition drive in Mumbai that has left more than 80,000 people homeless.[10] But apart from displacement in terms of habitation there are also other, more metaphoric kinds of displacement, such as the active displacement of the memories of certain events in the riots in the interest of restoring every day life. What are the stakes that people have in continuing to live in places where they have been victims of communal violence? An answer to this question would entail a re-examination of the culture of slum colonies. Slums are typically described as spaces of urban disintegration, places at the margins where the state has abandoned its civic responsibilities.[11] Slums are inherently unstable dwelling sites in which displacement is a fact of life.[12] Violence is not just a feature of communal strife but is part of the

---

[9] See Mehta's "Documents and Testimony: Violence, Witnessing and Subjectivity in the Bombay Riots – 1992-93" in this volume for a reading of the master narrative of the communal riot.

[10] This demolition drive began in December 2004 and ended in February 2005. It was ordered by the Chief Minister of Maharashtra, Vilas Rao Deshmukh, who heads a coalition government formed jointly by the Congress (I) and the National Congress Party (NCP). The demolitions were a first step in a Rs. 31,500 crore project to refurbish Mumbai ("Singapore in Mumbai," *Indian Express*, 26 February 2005, Mumbai edition).
   There are also connections between the two events of displacement. Thus victims of the riots who had been settled in a slum – Azminagar in Malwani, Mumbai – were displaced again when their huts were demolished in 2005 ("Doubly Displaced," *Mid Day*, 19 February 2005, Mumbai edition).

[11] AR Desai (ed.), *Expanding Governmental Lawlessness and Organizational Struggle* (Bombay: Popular Prakashan, 1991), Loic Wacquant, "America as Social Dystopia," in Pierre Bourdieu et al, *The Weight of the World: Social Suffering in Contemporary Society* (Cambridge: Polity Press, 1999), 110-120.

[12] Kalpana Sharma, "Introduction" in Nirmala Niketan, College of Social Work, *Bombay Mohalla Committees: A Case Study* (unpublished manuscript, 1997), 1-3.

inherent instability of everyday life.[13] But slums are also places of hope for its residents. Slum dwellers stake a claim to the city of Mumbai and aspire to a future within it. As residents of slums in Mumbai they come to acquire a public presence and find a collective voice.[14]

In the slums of Mumbai, NGOs have played an important role in the constitution of the 'slum voice.' They have supported efforts to organize at the local level and through their intervention many community-based organizations (henceforth CBOs) have developed cultures of democracy.[15] The significance of such CBOs has been acknowledged by the state. The most recent expression of this acknowledgement is the setting up of ward committees for participatory development in Mumbai in which CBOs find a place as representatives of the people.[16] Earlier, after the 1992-93 riots, the police in Mumbai sought the help of the NGOs and CBOs working in the slums in setting up *mohalla* (neighbourhood) committees. An important function of these committees was to anticipate and deflect future events of violence. Thus in 1995 there was a fear that the release of the feature film *Bombay* on the communal riots of 1992-93 would lead to riots in the city. The *mohalla* committees worked with the police and ensured that no events of violence took place after the film was released.[17] NGOs and CBOs have played an important role in the restoration of daily-ness in the slums of Mumbai after the violence of 1992-93 but this has been done not so much by confronting the trauma inflicted by violence but rather by deflecting it in the interest of achieving peace.

Jeffrey Alexander says that the construction of cultural trauma implies not only an identification of the existence and the

---

[13] Communal violence also leaves its shadow on the future. Thus many Muslim families in Dharavi, a slum in Mumbai where I have been doing fieldwork for the last 10 years, temporarily left Mumbai during the Gujarat riots of 2002, in anticipation that there might be a recurrence of violence in Mumbai.

[14] Arjun Appadurai, *Modernity at Large: Cultural Dimensions of Globalization* (Delhi: Oxford University Press, 1997). See also Chatterji, 'Plans,' p.5.

[15] Chatterji, 'Plans,' p.9.

[16] For purposes of administration Mumbai is divided into wards. Even though slums are present in most of the wards. G-North ward has a large number of them. The 74th amendment to the Indian Constitution has given more power to governance at the municipal level by encouraging decentralization and participatory planning.

[17] Sharma, *Introduction.*

source of social suffering but also the acknowledgement of responsibility for it.[18] Conversely, the denial of the other's suffering may also
be a refusal to participate in the social life of the other. Communal
riots in India, as Mehta's paper in this volume shows, have typically
been characterized as spontaneous occurrences and the memories
associated with such events have to be set aside for normal life to
resume. In spite of their self-presentation as the conscience-keepers of
society, NGOs sometimes share moral responsibility in the construction of such images of communal violence. I do not mean that NGOs
actively collude with the state in trying to legitimize particular acts of
violence. It is precisely because many of the NGOs who work in
slum areas are deeply embedded within local communities, that they
understand the condition of 'radical uncertainty'[19] that marks everyday life in slums and are aware that the state is the owner of the fundamental resources necessary for survival such as water, land and
sanitation.[20] An involvement with slum communities is thought inevitably, to lead to an involvement with the state. However it also
means that as far as events of collective violence is concerned, no
resolution is sought to be achieved. Its effects are dispersed in everyday life, marking day-to-day transactions involving work and livelihood. Thus some of the Muslim families who had come back to
Dharavi after the riots complained that networks of credit that had
formerly included both Muslim and Hindu businessmen had now
shrunk and become exclusively Muslim. Similarly some informants
would complain that if one had a Muslim name it took longer to get
official documents like ration cards renewed. This effect was felt

---

[18] Jeffrey C. Alexander, "Towards a Theory of Cultural Trauma," in Jeffrey Alexander
et al., *Cultural Trauma and Collective Identity* (Berkeley: University of California
Press, 2004), 1-30.

[19] I have borrowed this phrase from Achille Mbembe. I find that his portrayal of
conditions in Africa is similar to the slum communities that I am familiar with in
Mumbai and other parts of India. He uses this term to characterize the experience of
living in many worlds simultaneously, some of which are real and others false or
illusory. The juxtaposition of the two creates tremendous uncertainty as the subjects
caught up in these kinds of situations never know in advance which world is the real
one. Slum dwellers in Mumbai often describe their experiences with the state in these
terms. See Achille Mbembe, "Subject and Experience" in Nadia Tazi (ed.), *Keywords:
Experience* (New Delhi: Vistaar Publications, 2004): 1-18.

[20] Sunder Burra, *Cities Alliance Project on Pro-poor Slum Upgrading. Framework for
Mumbai*. Draft Report 2004 available at www.Sparcindia.org/documents/

even within voluntary organizations and CBOs. The Peoples' Organization for a Responsible Dharavi (PROUD), a CBO working exclusively in Dharavi, has still not recovered from the fact that two of its members, both residents of Dharavi, actually participated in the violence and the looting during the riots. My aim in trying to re-contextualize the riots is an attempt to understand the way in which the violence of 1992-93 becomes embedded in everyday life.

In this essay I argue that voluntary organizations like NGOs can be viewed as 'assemblages' – multiply-located within different sectors of society such that they pose negotiations between these sectors in new and ever changing ways. The contradictions that emerge in their self-identity are two of the many faces of the NGO as it mediates between the state and civil society.[21] Since my main concern in this essay is with slum redevelopment schemes in Mumbai, I am interested in the way in which NGOs become vectors, bringing modes of knowledge and organization from the sphere of government to the domain of everyday life in the slum. Some may argue that it is inappropriate to apply the concept of civil society to slum populations. Partha Chatterjee makes a distinction between civil and political society.[22] The former is the sphere of legality where the government reveals its face through norms and regulations, where the discourse of rights and citizenship can be meaningfully articulated. The latter is its dark underside – the sphere of illegality – where non-legitimate modes of doing are the norm. This is the sphere in which political negotiations, hustling and pressure tactics are common resources used to achieve a fragile stability. This according to Chatterjee is the kind of society a majority of Indians, certainly slum dwellers, experience on a day-to-day basis.[23]

In a previous work I have argued that it is not possible to posit Chatterjee's distinction between civil and political society as an empirical one. Slum-dwellers, inhabitant's of 'political society' in Chatterjee's terms, have far more at stake in issues relating to citizenship and civil rights than most middle-class Indians do on a daily

---

[21] Chatterji, Slum, p.10. See also Mendoza & D'Souza *The Long Winding Road, passim.*
[22] Partha Chatterjee, *The Politics of the Governed. Reflections on Popular Politics in Most of the World* (Delhi: Permanent Black, 2004).
[23] Ibid.

basis. However, I do think that one can think of this schema as referring to a juxtaposition of different spheres. Thus NGO practice can itself be thought of as an agonistic field or a vector for contestation and negotiation with governmental and political agencies. NGOs have the transformative potential to bridge the gap between civil and political society. This potential emerges, as Rabinow says, not so much from regulated participation in civil society but rather from "relatively chaotic sets of multiple opportunities and interdependencies."[24]

Critical Events and NGO Formation

The accounts that NGOs produce about themselves often privilege unique events that have had powerful social effects. These events become the 'conditions of possibility' for some future development – in this case for the self-institutionalization of NGOs. Thus events like the mass eviction of slum dwellers in 1980-81, the Prime Minister's Grant Project (PMGP) for Dharavi's development of 1985, the riots in 1992-93 and the 'Free Scheme' in 1995, have all been responsible in different ways for the way in which NGOs perceive themselves vis-à-vis slum populations. The one feature that these seemingly disparate events have in common is that they all lead to the *perception* of destabilization and mass displacement initiated by the state. This is followed by an *immediate* response from the *public* in the form of massive mobilization to resist these actions.[25] They also have had long-term institutional effects in that many of the NGOs that I discuss here developed federated structures – that is, networks and alliances with other organizations - to resist such forms of state intervention. Side-by-side with the growth of institutional networks is the perception that slum dwellers need to organize themselves into communities, to develop a public voice that will be heard by governments and by the larger population. As Sheela Patel, the charismatic head of one of the most influential NGOs working in this field, has said, the two must develop in tandem for the slum

---

[24] Paul Rabinow, *Anthropos Today* (Berkeley: University of California Press, 2003), 24.
[25] Rudolf Heredia, *Settlements and Shelter* (Report of the Committee for the Rights to Housing, 1985).

voice to be heard.[26] Paradoxically, NGO efforts to organize slum communities often mimic the very techniques of governmentality used by the state. Thus, some NGOs began to conduct surveys of slum and pavement dwellers that were in danger of being displaced in the 1980s. Aptly titled *We The Invisible,* this report is based on the survey of pavement dwellers conducted by Society for the Promotion of Area Resource Centres (henceforth SPARC). It prepared the ground for the emergence of a category of people whom the state would have no option but to acknowledge in the future.

Veena Das has coined the phrase 'critical event" to characterize moments that rupture the fabric of everyday life, in that their effects alter the way in which social relationships are conceived.[27] Thus this concept allows her to look at everyday life not from the perspective of the routine but from the shadow cast upon it by the extraordinary event. Das does not refer to his work in *Critical Events* but she may have had in mind the work of the great American sociologist G. H. Mead's formulation of the 'emergent event.' These are events and actions that are of such significance that they alter the way in which social life is organized.

In this section I shall explore one such event – the large-scale demolition of slum settlements in 1980-81 and its significance for the re-orientation of NGO activity especially in terms of long-term involvement in slum re-development. In the process I also hope to establish a different genealogy for the riots of 1992-93. As Mehta's essay in this volume shows, embedding the events of 1992-93 in the "communal riot narrative" gives them a sense of inevitability and self-explanation. It assumes that communal violence is a feature of Indian social life. Instead the genealogical method emphasizes the unique and contingent nature of events.[28] I hope to achieve this effect by placing different events of violence on the same page as it were.

In 1980, the Congress (Indira) government in Maharashtra, led by the Chief Minister, A. R. Antuley, ordered the mass eviction of

---

[26] Discussed in *We the Invisible Revisited* – SPARC document downloaded from www.sparcindia.org on 20 Sep 2003. See also Richard Burnham, *Community Action Planning* (Mumbai: YUVA Books, 2002).

[27] Veena Das, *Critical Event.* (Delhi: Oxford University Press, 1995).

[28] Michel Foucault, *Language, Counter-Memory, Practice. Selected Essays and Interviews* (Ithaca: Cornell University Press, 1977).

pavement dwellers from the city of Mumbai. Responding to the large number of petitions against this move that were filed in the courts, the Supreme Court ordered a stay on the so-called "Operation Demolition." However, in 1985, the stay order was evicted, following the judgment of the Supreme Court that declared the use of pavements for the purpose of shelter, illegal.[29] 1985 was also the year when the first two major projects for slum renewal were implemented – the PMGP for Dharavi and the World Bank sponsored SUP (Slum Upgradation Programme). Earlier, "Operation Demolition" of 1980-81 coincided with the appointment of a High Powered Steering Committee to study the problem of slum areas in 1981. Similarly Vilas Rao Deshmukh, the current chief minister of Maharashtra, ordered demolitions at a time when the Slum Rehabilitation Authority (SRA) was in the process of implementing large-scale rehabilitation schemes in Mumbai's slums. Thus, any act of positive intervention by the state, any effort to formalize and legitimize the state's relationship with a portion of its slum population is accompanied by another act that renders another part of this population non-legitimate. As Foucault has said, dividing practices form an important part of the process of governmentality.[30] They occur side by side with the technologies of power/ knowledge such as mapping and enumeration by which states make societies legible to themselves.

In the early 80s many of the NGOs who are now major players in the slum rehabilitation field acquired a public presence by taking a stance of active opposition to the state. Thus film personalities associated with Nivara Hakk Suraksha Samiti (Society for the Protection of Right to Shelter), like Shabana Azmi and Anil Patwardhan led mass demonstrations and hunger strikes in order to stop the demolitions.[31] SPARC followed a different approach as I have already said. They conducted a survey of pavement dwellers and according to their more recent report this exercise has led to the inclusion of pavement dwellers as an official category in the SRA.[32]

---

[29] Heredia, *Settlements*, 29.

[30] Michel Foucault, *Discipline and Punish: The Birth of the Prison.* (New York: Vintage, 1995).

[31] " Shabana Breaks Fast," *The Daily,* 14 May 1986, Bombay edition

[32] Burra, *Cities Alliance*, p.3. See also Afzulpurkar, Dinesh K. *Programme for the Rehabilitation of Slum and Hutment Dwellers in Brihan Mumbai* (Report of the

Also recent statements by Deshmukh, after the 2004-5 demolitions, that the state government will undertake a census of all slums that have come up after 1995, may also have its roots in the high profile surveys produced not just by SPARC but by other NGOs as well.[33] Such surveys are not merely important tools for producing knowledge about slum populations but are also thought to generate community participation as NGOs emphasize research *with* slum dwellers rather than merely gathering information *about* them.[34] In this connection it is also worth mentioning that many such voluntary organizations also feel that this kind of research is important in supporting the government's development role in this time of transition. They feel that this will "strengthen civil society and promote social development through local governance."[35]

Governmental Technologies and the Public Voice

From the first slum census in Mumbai in 1976, enumeration is an activity conducted on a regular basis in slums in which non-governmental organizations have a significant presence. To understand what this means let me describe the process by which this enumeration is conducted. I refer to a report by SPARC that also has a base in Dharavi.[36] This report describes enumeration as a "technology for community mobilization" and divides the activity into a number of stages. The first is called "hut counting." This takes place when members of the organization visit the slum area for the first time. As part of the activity of holding meetings with residents, they, together with some residents begin to mark the doors of houses with chalk. Residents are made aware that this is the first step towards

---

Study group appointed by the Government of Maharashtra for the Rehabilitation of Slum and Hutment Dwellers through Reconstruction, 1995).

[33] One such NGO is the Youth for Unity and Voluntary Action (YUVA), which has produced a series of surveys on several slum areas in Mumbai. Deshmukh's statement about a new survey follows an announcement about a new policy to rehabilitate slum dwellers occupying structures that have come up between 1995 and 2000. (Mumbai 21 Feb 2005), source - news.newkerela.com/india?action= fullnews&-id-75899.

[34] Burnham, *Community Action Planning*, p.19.

[35] Study on Citizens Participation in YUVA 1998 Global Transition Local Democracy: The Case of Mumbai, India. A Case Urban Governance (YUVA. unpublished report, 1998), 8.

[36] SPARC, *We The Invisible Revisited* (2004). See www.sparcindia.org

mapping the settlement. They begin to think about the criteria involved in establishing numbers for their houses and in the boundaries between their houses. (This is important because slum dwellings grow over time and it is often difficult to decide where one hut stops and another begins.) The report emphasizes that a dialogue must be allowed to develop around enumeration so that residents become conscious of their property rights and entitlements. Residents also do the next stage, "rough mapping" of the settlement. This is supposed to help them translate their experience of place (habitation) into an abstract spatial category. The third phase, "numbering," involves the matching of house number with the map. The chalk numbers are re-done in paint. After this stage, official surveyors take over. Residents are made aware that they have a responsibility regarding accurate self-reporting since this process will be repeated and any claim that they may have to municipal or state services will be evaluated through these surveys. However, as the report says, self-surveys have another equally important role. They make slum dwellers aware of a new identity based on abstract citizenship rather than on more ascriptive features like caste and religion.

One could read this exercise in self-enumeration in two ways – either as the internalization and normalization of a disciplinary regime: or as a way of creating a new self-identity on the basis of universal rights.[37] Developing on this theme, Benedict Anderson (1998) makes a distinction between 'bound' and 'unbound seriality.'[38] The former creates totalities like population (through the census); the latter is open-ended and additive, creating horizontal links with similar categories. Thus, for instance, concepts like '*a* nation' and '*a* citizen' are based on the principle of universality. They involve the activity of addition. They are open to the world as they form a common basis to community. NGOs like SPARC would probably say that forms of bounded seriality also work with the principle of universality since it enables slum dwellers to develop global links with similarly placed groups. Initial self-enumeration exercises were responses to particular events like the 1980-81 mass demolitions. It

---

[37] Foucault, *Discipline and Punish, passim.*
[38] Benedict Anderson, *The Spectre of Comparisons: Nationalism, Southeast Asia and the World* (London: Verso, 1998).

made the slum-dwellers visible to the state. The census itself can become an event. This was the case with the 1976 slum census since it had the capacity to re-define the status of a slum dweller into that of a potential citizen. On this occasion, slum dwellers that had been enumerated were given 'photo-passes' which gave official recognition to them as residents of a particular notified slum. Since then this cut-off date has been extended several times. Thus, if we think of the census operation as an event – it points to contradictory processes at work within this attempt at containing the slum population. Instead, it opens a new field of negotiation, so that the date, which is supposed to fix the population and provide closure, is constantly being deferred.[39] Cut-off dates also draw voluntary organizations to the state's field of practice. Politicians, the state and CBOs, to strengthen support from local slum communities, use negotiations over cut-off dates as a resource. This makes it difficult to think of slum dwellers as forming a single homogeneous community. Cut-off dates operate both as a dividing practice produced by the state to govern the body population but also as a tool for creating a space for negotiations with the state.

Slum Housing: A Fundamental Right or a Commodity in the Market?

The field of slum housing is one of the most politicized issues in Mumbai – with some of the major players being the government, the NGOs and the builders' lobby. Each of these three sectors articulates a different view regarding the slum population of Mumbai. The fundamental opposition is based on a clash of principles – is housing a fundamental right or a commodity? NGOs have used the discourse of human rights – shelter as a fundamental right for all – to frame

---

[39] Foucault says that, "an event is not a decision...but a reversal of a relationship of forces...the appropriation of a vocabulary turned against those who had once used it. (Foucault, *Language, Counter-Memory, Practice*, p.146.). The tactic of deferral is a resource that can be used by politicians as well. Reports on the NGO PROUD (People's Organization for a United Dharavi), from the 1980s say that the PMGP almost destroyed PROUD's ability to work in Dharavi. There was an anticipation that it would introduce divisiveness within the slum population so that PROUD would no longer be able to speak for all of Dharavi's residents. PROUD claims that its status as the slum voice and its strategy of opposition has brought about a change in the state's perception as revealed in its policies of slum-redevelopment.

their activities in the slums of Mumbai. However, since the early 90s, with the inception of the 'Free Scheme' (officially, "Slum Re-development Programme or SRD), and the involvement of the private sector in slum re-habilitation work, slums in Mumbai are increasingly being viewed as "organizational commodities."[40] Slums like Dharavi that were once on the outskirts of the city have now been integrated within its commercial space and are considered to be commercially lucrative sites for development. It is assumed that once these slum dwellers become legitimate home owners and are treated as citizens by the state they will also enter the money economy as tax paying citizens.[41] Dharavi's residents are being transformed from being destitute migrants who have no legitimate status in the city to dynamic entrepreneurs capable of contributing to Mumbai's culture and economy. I will have more to say on this transformation later but clearly as the recent demolitions of 2004-05 show, not all slum colonies are viewed as sites of commercial growth.

The recent demolition drive was also inspired by an economic vision for the city. *Vision Mumbai,* a report produced in 2003 by 'Bombay First,' an independent body whose members consist of corporate heads and many of Mumbai's prominent citizens, appointed a consultancy form, McKinsey & Co. to draft a proposal for Mumbai's makeover which has been accepted by the state government. The report proposes a re-development plan for the city in keeping with its status as the financial capital of India. With a proposed budget of Rs. 31,000 crores, plans have been made for large infrastructure projects such as metro rail links, trans-harbours, state-of-the-art flyovers, ring railways and upgraded airports. It also recommends that the current slum population of Mumbai, which is approximately 50-60%, be reduced to 10-20% as slums pose a heavy

---

[40] Saskia Sassen talks about the "city as a site for new claims by global capital" in Saskia Sassen, "Whose City Is It? Globalization and the Formation of New Claims," *Public Culture* (8), 1996: 205-223. The 'Free Scheme' that was conceived in 1995 proposed that the charge of building the tenements would be given to private builders who would build free flats for slum dwellers in exchange for land on which they could build flats for sale (Chatterji, 'Plans', p.15). However proposals for public-private partnership for slum development work have been mooted from the early 80s (see *Report of the High power Steering Group for Slums and Dilapidated Houses* (1981), headed by Ajit Kerkar, a representative of the private sector).
[41] " Slum Dewellers Entrepreneurs" *Economic Times*, 8 Mar 2004.

burden on the city's infra-structure.[42] As an initial step in the implementation of this plan, the Chief Minister of Maharashtra decided to demolish all slums that had come up in Mumbai after the official cut-off date of 1995.[43] Slums that cannot be integrated into the larger plan for the city must be demolished.

How have these demolitions affected state/ NGO relations? Important NGOs like SPARC and its alliance partners[44] and Nivara Hakk Suraksha Samiti are involved in large rehabilitation projects for slum dwellers that will be ousted by development schemes such as the World Bank funded Mumbai Urban Transport Project. They have also been vocal in their protest against the recent demolitions.[45] However, most voluntary organizations working in slum areas intend to carry on working *with* rather than *against* the government. Thus, to quote from SPARC's annual report, "the alliance sees itself as an institution within civil society, with a role to act as both gadfly and partner to state agencies..."[46] In accordance with its role as conscience keeper of the state it has designed strategies to make demands on state agencies, to change government policies and so on. It has formalized this form of strategizing by naming it 'precedent-setting.' Among the victories that it has achieved with this mode of strategizing, is the official recognition of pavement dwellers by the SRA. It views this achievement as a direct result of its ongoing work with pavement dwellers and the census it conducted among them in the 80s after the 1981 demolitions. Another achievement is the creation of new housing structures in the Markandeya Cooperative Society in Dharavi, which were finally given official recognition more than a decade after the inception of the project but did lead to changes being made in the development control regulations in the

---

[42] " Mumbai Makeover" *The Telegraph*, 3 Jun 2005, Calcutta edition.

[43] According to official sources there are approximately 1.5 lakh hutments that have come up between 1995 and 2000 which house around eight lakh persons (Cited in "Mumbai's New Look," *New Kerela*, 25 Feb 2005, Mumbai edition).

[44] SPARC has an 'alliance' with Mahila Milan (an organization of pavement dwellers) and the National Slum Dwellers Federation.

[45] See *Midday*, 1 February 2005, Mumbai edition, for an interview on the recent demolitions with Shabana Azmi – Member of Parliament-Rajya Sabha and chairperson of Nivara Hakk Suraksha Samiti.

[46] SPARC, *We the Invisible*, 29.

city of Mumbai.[47] Off course 'precedent-setting' – "the negotiation between the legalities of urban government and illegal arrangements to which the poor almost always have to resort"[48] – is possible only over an extended period of time. The endeavours of the Alliance in both these cases took over a decade to achieve official recognition.[49] SPARC however, sees this as one of the consequences of its critical engagement with the state. I quote, "state bashing alone is not enough... all the goods that poor people need – land, water, sanitation, electricity, housing finance and so on are regulated by state agencies...At least the State is accountable in principle in democratic theory, however weak the mechanisms to hold it accountable might be..."[50] Also, "We (the Alliance) have taken a conscious decision to interact with all manner of institutions – including the World Bank and public and private financial institutions – in order to influence them through a conversation that includes the voices of the poor."[51]

This changing vision of state/ society relations must also include a new vision of slums and its residents. A perusal of newspaper reports about slums like Dharavi over the last decade depicts them as sites for commerce and industry and for "popular capital formation and economic growth."[52] Thus, U.R. Bhatt talks about the "democratization of capital" and the importance of legalizing property rights in slums like Dharavi for the growth of capitalist economy.[53] He says that for slum dwellers to be recognized as citizens who can be organized into "a network of individually identifiable and accountable business agents" the law needs to be aware of how "people define,

---

[47] The Markandeya Housing Cooperative Society was formed under the auspices of the Prime Minister's Grant Project of 1985 and was supported by the Alliance. It decided to construct houses with fourteen foot high walls in accordance with the architecture of Dharavi in which many permanent constructions have lofts to extend the living space. At that time development control regulations only permitted walls of a height of nine and a half feet. See Vinit Mukhija, *Squatters as Developers? Slum Redevelopment in Mumbai* (Hampshire: Ashgate Publishing, 2003) and SPARC, *We the Invisible*, 35.
[48] Arjun Appadurai, "Deep Democracy: Urban Governmentality and the Horizon of Politics," *Public Culture* 14(1), 2002: 21-48, 34.
[49] Mukhija, *Squatters*, 17.
[50] SPARC, *We the Invisible*, 29.
[51] Burra, *Cities Alliance*, p.41.
[52] UR Bhatt, director, JP Morgan, India, in the *Economic Times*, 8 Mar 2004, Mumbai edition.
[53] Ibid.

use and distribute property rights." Title deeds to property will free its economic features and transform property into an asset capable of wider circulation as capital. Bhatt makes the point that property claims already function in this way. But because these transactions operate in the informal or extra-legal sector they are restricted to narrow, local circles where people know and trust each other.

NGOs like SPARC and its partners have also experimented with micro-credit schemes among women pavement dwellers and with small investor funds in collaboration with the Unit Trust of India.[54] However, what is more important from the point of view of this paper is the fact that the significance of translocal networks is emphasized in disparate discourses. Thus Sheela Patel speaks of knowledge and experience generated at the local level being transformed into social capital once it is exchanged with communities of similarly placed people across the globe. This capital can, in turn, be used as a resource for change at the level of state policy not just at the local or national level, but internationally as well.[55]

On the face of it the discourse of commoditization and the discourse of human rights occupy very different moral positions. Unlike commodities, rights are non-alienable and non-transferable. However, in one respect at least, they do have something in common. Commodities and rights both represent abstract values that can be conceptualized as generalized media of exchange that come to acquire their symbolic value by participating in well developed cultures of circulation.[56] Markets, the context in which commodities circulate, and the human rights discourse are both transnationally located. In this aspect they provide avenues for the expression of freedom and distantiation from the constraints of local context. The role of the market and of money in the generalization of value and thus in the freeing of the individual from particularistic social bonds are well

---

[54] The Unit Trust of India is a financial organization sponsored by the government. See also SPARC *We the Invisible*, p.31.

[55] Paper presented by Sheela Patel at a conference on 'Globalization North/South. Social Movements and New Social Communities' organized by the International Sociological Association on 20.4.2001. See also, Sheela Patel, Joel Bolnick, Diana Mitlin 2001 "Creating and Strengthening an International Voice for the Urban Poor." (www.sparcindia.org) (1-14)

[56] LH Mayhew (ed.), *Talcott Parsons on Institutions and Social Evolution* (Chicago: University of Chicago Press, 1982).

known.[57] However, as Rabinow says, the authoritative universalism within which the language of rights is articulated is a way of expressing one's freedom from one's local cultural identity.[58] Self identity is freed from its specific social context with its complement of social roles such as 'illegal resident,' 'migrant' and so on. The human rights discourse allows for the expression of abstract identity, a dimension recognized by NGOs like SPARC that speak of 'widening and deepening' the slum dwellers voice by linking it to similarly placed people in other parts of the world.[59] Even NGO's with very localized identities like PROUD partake of this translocal discourse. Apart from organizing workshops and seminars in Dharavi on the occasion of transnational events like the *International Year for the Shelter of the Homeless* in 1987, even the reports of its 'issue based' committees that deal with specific local issues are framed in the language of human rights. Thus, the report of PROUD's drainage committee in 1983 concludes its account by referring to Dharavi's contribution to the strengthening of industry and commerce in Mumbai as well as to human rights generally and through the labour of PROUD's members who represent the people of Dharavi.[60]

Clearly, representations of slum dwellers as agents of social change, of capacity building and economic growth in slums are dispersed on different sites of production. One could say that 'new' localities (i.e. slum colonies) are being produced through the circulation of these discourses.[61] Lee and Lipuma argue that the phenomenon of circulation is more than the mere movement of ideas and commodities from one sphere to another.[62] Rather it produces its own culture embedded in systems of self-reflexivity, abstraction, evaluation and constraint.[63] These cultures of circulation interpene-

[57] George Simmel, *Philosophy of Money* (London: Routledge & Kegan Paul, 1978).
[58] Rabinow, *Anthropos Today*, 108.
[59] SPARC, *We the Invisible*, 42.
[60] PROUD, *Annual Report* (1983), 87.
[61] Appadurai, *Modernity*, 201. Even though the market is one of the more important traditional sites of circulation, workshops and conferences have emerged as new sites of circulation especially through the proliferation of NGO activity.
[62] Benjamin Lee & Edward Lipuma, "Cultures of Circulation: The Imaginations of Modernity," *Public Culture* 14 (1), 2002, 191-214.
[63] Dilip Parameshwar Gaonkar,,"Towards New Imaginaries: An Introduction," *Public Culture* 14(1), 2002, 1-20.

trate thereby facilitating the "sedimentation of particular representations of collective agency and community formation" as we have seen. However, once NGOs start becoming developers, once the state, the market and the NGOs work along parallel lines what will happen to the voice of the urban poor? I have shown in a previous paper, slum dwellers acquire a public voice through the conflicts between the representatives of different interests in the field and the contradictions between different forms of legality and legitimacy.[64] Modern forms of sociality, forms that are self-constituted, based on systems of self-reflexivity require the friction produced by conflicting value systems.[65] NGOs are certainly modern forms of sociality, self institutionalized in the context of discussions about new values, protests and "repression based on force."[66] Will they be able to sustain, even re-invent themselves, without the oppositional stance to the state and to the market?

Finally, let us return to the riots of 1992-93. As far as Dharavi is concerned, this marks the first time that communal violence made an impact on the slum. However, in spite of the fact that the influence of trace memories of the event are seen in such phenomena as the short term migration out of Dharavi and even Mumbai during the Gujarat riots of 2002, (described as a precautionary measure by some Muslim residents), the memorialization of victimhood does not take place. This is in stark contrast to the situation described in Yasmeen Arif's paper in this volume, for instance. The widows of Tilak Vihar, victims of the 1984 anti-Sikh riots in Delhi, think of themselves as a 'community of martyrs' according to Arif. Their subjectivity is shaped by the experience of a failed justice system and through the embracing of the problematic category of victimhood. For most slum dwellers in Mumbai, the espousal of such an identity is problematic, precisely because there is no single event of violence that configures their relationship with the state. Rather, everyday life in the slum is lived in the shadow of state violence. However, the state also has an enabling face, one that I have tried to describe in this paper. This is represented not so much through its re-

---

[64] Chatterji, 'Slums,' p.29.
[65] Joas, *Mead*, page ref.
[66] Joas, *Mead*, 209.

development and rehabilitation policies and schemes that carry the potential of enormous violence as I have shown but through the un-intended consequences of the documentary practices that accompany such schemes. Practices such as the slum census have enabled slum populations to acquire a new identity and a public voice.[67] However, without the mediating presence of NGOs, the constitution of this new identity would not have been possible.

Roma Chatterji *is a Reader in Sociology, Delhi School of Economics, University of Delhi. She has published on collective violence, slum housing, folklore and the medicalization of illness experience in the Netherlands.*

---

[67] Appadurai 2004, Chatterji 2003

www.ingramcontent.com/pod-product-compliance
Lightning Source LLC
Chambersburg PA
CBHW031516270326
41930CB00006B/422